SIX

POETRY WINTER 2015

SIXFOLD
WWW.SIXFOLD.ORG

Sixfold is a collaborative, democratic, completely writer-voted journal. The writers who upload their manuscripts vote to select the prize-winning manuscripts and the short stories and poetry published in each issue. All participating writers' equally weighted votes act as the editor, instead of the usual editorial decision-making organization of one or a few judges, editors, or select editorial board.

Each issue is free to read online, to download as PDF and as an e-book for iPhone, Android, Kindle, Nook, and others. Paperback book is available at production cost including shipping.

© The Authors. No part of this document may be reproduced or transmitted without the written permission of the author.

Cover Art by Peter Rawlings. *Collage of a man in a chair.* 2009. Paper and glue. 3" x 7" http://peterrawlings.com

SIXFOLD   GARRETT DOHERTY, PUBLISHER
28 FARM FIELD RIDGE ROAD   SANDY HOOK CT 06482
SIXFOLD@SIXFOLD.ORG   WWW.SIXFOLD.ORG   (203) 491-0242

SIXFOLD

POETRY WINTER 2015
CONTENTS

J. H Yun
Sundays for the Faithful II … 9
Yesenia (Castro Valley's Jane Doe) … 10

Colby Hansen
The Lepidopterist … 11
Under Glass, Inside a Frame … 13
The Killing Jars … 14
Killing Jar #37 … 15
Slipknot … 17

Melissa Bond
Confession … 18
Hush … 19
Mint Leaf for David Foster Wallace … 20
Now You See It … 22
Freud's Asparagus … 23

Jane Schulman
Final Crescent … 24
When Krupa Played Those Drums … 25
Overheard on the F Train … 27
Back and Forth … 28
After … 29

Susan F. Glassmeyer
Hercules Visits My Kitchen … 30
Seeing Movement … 31
While Holding a Shivering Toad in My Hands … 32
First Moon of a Blue Moon Month … 33
Parting Word … 34

Melissa Tyndall
For Our Children, Not Yet Born,
    I Preserve the Images of Animals   35
Postcards from the Amer River   36
Haptics   37
Film Studies   38
Aubade   39

Micah Chatterton
Medicine   40
Kin   42
A Love Poem   43
Dropped Tanka   44

Emily Graf
Toolbox   45
Photograph of Two Girls Outside Crazy Horse,
    South Dakota (2007)   46
2AM Instagram of Lunar Eclipse   47
Striking Matches   48

Kate Magill
NOLA, 2006   50
Morning, Five Ways   51
Tanka for The New Year   53
LV Winter, 2015   54

Michael Fleming
Desire   55
Khao-I-Dang   56
Lunch   57
The Voice of America   58
Meeting Mrs Ping   59

Richard Parisio
On a Photograph Taken in Newark, 1929   60
Brown Creeper   61
Mentor   62
Triumphal   63
The Honey Seeker   65

Jennifer Leigh Stevenson
Honey I'm Headed West   66
Undone   68
The Dangers of Prose, Love   69
Circe in Business   70
Quarry   72

Laurel Eshelman
Tuckpointing   73
Home Game   74
Outpatient   75
You Call Me to Jump   76

Barry W. North
The Molotov Cocktail of the Deep South   77
The First Day   79
All That Glitters   81
Thanks   82
You Are Also What You Don't Do   83

Charles C. Childers
Camouflage   84
Privilege   85
Recessive   86
Underseam   87
Synchronized   88

Ricky Ray
Listening   89
The Crossroads a Pound of Flesh Is   91
Quiet, Grit, Glory   92
A Way to Work   94
Poems That Are Poems Even Though They Aren't Poems, I Swear It   97

Cassandra Sanborn
Bird Watching   98
Last Night   100
Botany Lessons   102
Older   103
Revelation   104

Linda Sonia Miller
- Eclipse — 105
- Kaida Does The Stomp — 106
- Full Circle — 107
- Delivery — 108
- The Weight of Birds — 109

J. Lee Strickland
- The Music of the Spheres — 110
- High Tide — 111
- How To Know The Grasses — 112
- Practice — 113
- Anna's Plague — 114

Erin Dorso
- March in Manarola — 115
- On the Drive Back to Andersonville — 116
- In the Kitchen — 117
- Fig Keeper — 118

Holly Lyn Walrath
- Behind the Glass — 119
- Housewife — 120
- She Learns How to Disappear — 121
- Two Young Wives — 122
- Aerie — 123

Jeff Lewis
- Charles Ives, a Connecticut Yankee — 124
- Berlioz Wins a Bride — 126
- Musak — 128
- Listening to Music — 130
- Wagner — 132

Karen Kraco
- Stuck — 133
- Postcard Poems: Animal Attitude — 134
- Rough Dreams — 136
- Shaker Village at Pleasant Hill — 137

Rafael Miguel Montes
    Gas Mask   138
    Broom   139
    Going Public   140
    Casket   141
    Mail   142

Contributor Notes   143

J.H Yun

Sundays for the Faithful II

They tear into the face of the gape mouthed mackerel,
dislodging the eyes and sharing them, unhinging the jaw so it hangs,
a flap of skin after a potato peeler mishap. I wonder about the assaulting
nature of winter. The way it comes and comes,
and seduction is a violence all its own. Did you drink from the fountain
you weren't supposed to yet? Even the dumbest of birds are struck
with the same madness that send them all careening south
balding the horizon in winter when the first snow falls
when the bud first bursts or is first burst.

When I was young I couldn't outrun my lisp or gap toothed whistle.
Outside the sky is curdling over, masking daddy's view of us,
and the stragglers with their frostbitten wings are thrown down
as if they were born for that. Inside, the boys corral the quiet ones
into the closet, undress them, prick bloodied initials on their flush
    pink skin.
Tells them *hush, Daddy's too busy spying on the neighbors to hear*
    you anyhow.

Yesenia (Castro Valley's Jane Doe)

Nine years old, we nose the gully's edge for flowers
to eat, pant legs rolled to tufts on our bug bitten calves.
Here, we fancy ourselves deer,

and like any good creature of prey, we cringe away from noise,
the mere suggestion of headlights groping the fog
at a distance we can't quite see over the creek's open mouth.

We feign fear, but only for fun. For whatever reason,
feeling hunted and liking it. When we come across a vine
of purple flowers, we linger.

Look, honeysuckles, I say, wrong though I don't know it yet,
and we pull the stems off the violet's head, lick the nectar
from the apex where the petals gather, suck until we are sated

and leave the gully as humans again. Now forget us.
Here comes the girl with the crown of chestnut hair
followed by a man, but he is not important.

She will lie with the violets for weeks before she's found,
nestled in a canvas bag like a chrysalis with a throatful of rags,
lovely in the police composite sketch,

she won't own a name for ten years. But the butterfly clip
in her hair confesses. Clinging to her despite river bed muck,
despite winter, despite cruel hands committing her body to
    earth,

its sweet, pink adornments insisting *She was a child, she*
    was a child,
while the bust made from a study of her bones smiles
soft through the static, right before we change the channel.

Colby Hansen

The Lepidopterist

I rap on the front screen door
and press my forehead
against the wire mesh to see inside—
smelling Pall Mall smoke
and hearing that dry creak of chains
from the porch swing dangling on the eave.
There, on the seat:
the *Echium Daily News*,
open to the obituaries
because the lepidopterist always starts her day
by checking to see if she made it through the night.

She had a stroke a few years back,
smoking Pall Mall cigarettes on the front porch—
one moment flicking burning ashes into the grass,
and the next:
pitching over the rail,
some little artery in her brain
erupting like an overfilled water balloon.
Only her left side survived.
Her right has been dead ever since.

The rubber tip of her polished, mahogany cane
meets the linoleum of the kitchen floor.
I listen to her approach:
the thump of her cane;
the drag of her leg;
the rasp of her breath.
Ithonia Brushfoot hobbles toward me
on a path etched into the carpet
like tire ruts on a dirt road.

Thump.
Drag.
Rasp.

It is as if the line between Heaven and earth
has been drawn down the middle of her body,
and after all this time
she still doesn't know which place she would rather be.
Lucky for me,
she cannot seem to leave Echium for good.

The lepidopterist,
you should probably know,
is the closest thing to a real friend I have.

Under Glass, Inside a Frame

She smiles her half-smile
and mumbles something ambiguous—
Hello, or, *Let's go*—
while I pause to inspect the clusters of butterflies
lining her living room walls.
They look so alive I am almost surprised
they don't flutter away when I stir them with my breath;
but these ones are dried and pinned—
because Ithonia Brushfoot seems to like them best
under glass, inside a frame.

You can't always tell what she is saying,
ever since the stroke
left her tongue lolling inside her lopsided mouth
and pushing out words like marbles
that half the time fall to the floor
and roll away as marbles sometimes do.

But once,
when I found an old brass-framed photograph
on a table beside her bed
and asked,
Is this YOU?
she nodded her head—
a little to the left,
as if she was jostling water from her ear—
and told me,
clear as day,
I wasn't always like this, dear.

The Killing Jars

Ithonia Brushfoot needs me
for everything that takes two hands to do—
cutting grass and changing pillowcases
or even the simplest things
you never knew
you couldn't do
with only one hand until you actually tried:
opening envelopes or bottles of aspirin
and twisting the lid off a tube of toothpaste,
a gallon of milk,
or any one of the thirty-six killing jars
the lepidopterist keeps lined up
on a shelf inside her garage.

There's a sun tea brewer, #9,
which smells of spearmint and chamomile
and is for the swallowtails so massive
you'd think their shadows were cast by birds;
and there's an apricot baby food jar, #23,
which fits perfectly inside the palm of your hand—
just like the tiny Colorado hairstreak.

Their cyanide-speckled cakes of sawdust and plaster
crumble like old cement at the bottom;
and Ithonia Brushfoot's wobbly,
old-fashioned handwriting labels each one—
permanent ink
on a single strip of masking tape
that time has curled and yellowed
into some stage of decay.

Thirty-six jars.
Thirty-six ways to smother a butterfly dead.

But don't try to convince her it's inhumane.
She'll just glare at you through her one good eye,
muttering something ambiguous like,
And what's YOUR hobby?
or,
Just try to stop me.

Killing Jar #37

Ithonia Brushfoot's garage
smells of stale Pall Mall smoke and poison—
and so I hold my breath,
like always,
making room on the workbench
littered with the tools of a lepidopterist:
straight pins and scissors;
tweezers;
screwdrivers;
rubber cement;
glass magnifying lenses.
And then there is Killing Jar #37—
a Strong Shoulder Mason
with a wide-open mouth and gritty zinc lid.
Quart-sized.
Smelling of dill.
Pickles, probably.

Ithonia Brushfoot glares at me
through her one good eye
as I measure out a single serving of crystalline cyanide.
A sharp, bitter smell wafts up around me
when I sprinkle it into the bottom of the jar.
More,
she orders,
leaning forward on her mahogany cane—
and so I add another pinch.
The truth is
the difference between one spoonful of poison
and two
doesn't mean a thing to a butterfly.

I've already peppered in a layer of sawdust
and a glob of gypsum plaster,
plus a sheet of crumpled tissue paper
to absorb moisture
and give her specimens a soft place to die.
Across the garage,

Ithonia Brushfoot nods—
a little to the left,
like always—
and the killing jar is complete.

I still get heartsick,
every time a butterflies dies.
What effect it has on Ithonia Brushfoot
is more of a mystery—
because ever since the stroke
you can only be sure of half
of what you think you see on her face.

Sometimes,
her eyes betray her guilt;
but then she ruins it
by mumbling something ambiguous—
something like,
Go find me some pins,
or,
Like you've never sinned.

Slipknot

I caught her today
with her nose inside the jar—
sniffing deep breaths
of poisonous fumes
and trying her best
not to cringe.
She heard me gasp;
hollered, *Don't sneak like that*!
or,
Go get my net!
and lit a cigarette
so she'd have a reason
to ventilate the space
now that she wasn't alone.

But I saw what I saw.

And so when I let
that terrible jar
slip like a knot
through the crook in my arm
it's on purpose—
I don't care
if she knows.

Melissa Bond

Confession

And finally, after months of this new baby, the oxygen tubes catching in the door frames, tripping us up at night, the fear like electricity cracking in our bedroom, finally you confess. We'd done a ritual. Purification. Consumption. Medicine. We vomited for hours in the sourdark. Singing. To hitch a ride on. Singing to pull out your demons. And the dreams came like hyperspace, like some loco driving in our heads. You dreamed crazy. Saw yourself in a crazy house, walking in and out of bodies, losing yourself. Like your mama did and probably her mama before her. A bindweed choking your family history. You had always been afraid of that weed, had always hacked at it with your machete, had spent your life running like a dog. It was later that you told me, after you'd returned, after your eyes lost their ghostliness. *When he was born,* you said, *I was afraid that it was me. I was afraid that you'd know that something was sour in me, the water was bad, that I was the one who shifted our boy's chromosomes. I was the one who made him slow.*

Hush

Before making my way into the intubated hush
of the Intensive Care Unit,
I pass a hallway of teenagers,
their spines pressed collectively against white walls, dark eyes
pinned to the long stretch of linoleum on which I'm walking.

The boy with a mass of tangled Afro glances
up as I pass, his eyes naked with the kind of vulnerability
that only comes from the wounded—did I know Her—
the girl with the gunshot wound to the head
who, my doctor friend would later tell me
would end her seventeen years on this earth
with bone fragments sprayed into the soft gel
of her brain, the hand forgetting it's a hand,
the heartbeat flying the caged coup
of the body.

I'm reminded of the time I watched my four-day-old
son stretched out on a warming slab in a Neonatal
Intensive Care Unit. His tiny hand lay palm up
under the lights, curled and red as a bird claw.
Standing there, my breasts sick with milk,
I saw his life counted out in measured beats
and felt each alarm as if it was my own—
my breath shortening with his, my heart slowing
as his dipped and swayed.

I'm amazed at how wounded we are with the sudden awareness
not of our own mortality, but of the ones we love.
Does it hurt?
Yes, it still hurts.
And back then I wanted it to keep hurting
because with each wound I'd feel that he was still alive,
as if I could be his Sisyphus, as if I could hold the suffering
for both of us so he'd take just one more breath,
just one more,
just another.

Mint Leaf for David Foster Wallace

Often there are times when I am staring off
into the skim line of horizon, where the soft peach
of sky folds into the earth's body,
and I find myself comparing my son
to David Foster Wallace.

I remember reading about Mr. Wallace's suicide,
about his parents knowing that there was something wrong
with their bright boy, about his starry rise
amongst the intellectual literati
and his depression so debilitating that, like Kafka,
the disease that tormented was life itself.

And I couldn't help feeling sad that in my love
of Wallace's brilliant articulations,
and my appreciation for his infinite, witty jests
I too had jumped up to clap my soft hands,
and did not see his overwhelming sadness.

And today, as I watch my two year-old son,
diagnosed with Down Syndrome at just five days old,
I can't help but wonder at the quality of *his* intelligence
and what he might have passed
on to Mr. Wallace? Because there are days
when I feel a particular loneliness
and I am tempted to recline into the cynic's
tattered and yellow-stained armchair to cast dispersions at life's
false pageantry, and to mutter perhaps, a diatribe or two about the state
of the world.

And on these days, I come home to my son,
who greets me just as he does on every other day,
lifting his small arms into the hallelujah air
and clapping fervently, as if I'd scored yet
another touchdown in our touchdown of days.

And when he crawls forward, stopping briefly
to thumb a mint leaf or to laugh himself to tears,

I bend, grateful for his arms around my neck,
grateful for the reminder that some forms of intelligence break
the world into pieces of beautiful ugliness,
and some do not break the world at all.

Now You See It

My mother cups my uterus
to her mouth and blows.
The uterine balloon she hangs
like a trophy in her bedroom,
nailed to the far wall like an animal
skin.

At parties she fills it with wine,
places a nozzle on it and pours.
The guests are enchanted. They tell me
what a good girl I am. How lucky
to have a mother so intimate. I tell
them that my mother loves
tricks, loves the jigsaw puzzle
of my spine, love to pull my heart
from her ear and make it disappear
into her mouth. What a mother, they say.
What a magician.
Soon, she'll be able to make you
disappear altogether.

Freud's Asparagus

She tries to sublimate
a hot Sunday at 8 a.m.,
but he pounds at her door,
repressed, Freudian
and hungry.

She cooks him sweet butter eggs
and asparagus
and he looks at her.
"Sometimes an asparagus is just
an asparagus," she says, placing
the green, feathery tip deep
into her mouth.

She hands him a swollen, red
plum, a fat, hairy peach.
She says, "Eat."
She says, "Read to me. Tell me of Plato's
Republic. I want to see a civilization come
from between your lips."

They practice sword fighting
in the garden. She has better footwork
but his shaft is longer, bright red
and she laughs at him.
He pins her again and again in the garden
with swollen red fruit and thick
leaves and she laughs at him.
He does not know what the woman wants.

She leads him to the bath.
"Here. Play with the toy boat—
the small fringed sails, the wet hull . . ."

He is nearly hysterical when she takes him
(as she knew she would)
and hours later, in the lingering flame of his sleeping body,
she smokes.

Jane Schulman

Final Crescent

Think of me on bruise-blue nights when
        moons wane to wisps
                and you scan the eastern sky.

Think of me as a crocus
        cracking through matted leaves.

For I was born on ebbing days
        of Adar, when winds blew out-of-tune
                and the moon a final crescent.

My soul makes its way through
        the world with hesitant footfalls.

Two of our sons were born in the month
        of Nissan. Prankish as lion cubs,
                hearts of honeycomb and voile.

I know my soul more by what it is not.

When Krupa Played Those Drums

Sometimes I can't think in metaphors.
Rocks are rocks. Tumors are tumors.

Time in close present.
10 tomorrow, CT scan.

I lie in bed. Listen for signs of life.
A cough. A snore.

By 2 AM clack of Dad's walker,
slipper-shuffle to the kitchen
for bourbon on ice.

9 AM He falls. I boost
from behind. He yanks

with still-strong arms
and he's on the sofa.

Victory when we don't
need to call 9-1-1.

9:45 He slips on his loafers.
Back in motion. We're off for the test..

5 PM He leans back in his chair,
stares at a black TV.

No Jeopardy. No C-Span.
Not even Ella Fitzgerald on the stereo.

What is it you think about, Dad,
while you sit with the TV off?

I go back to the good years
when I'd just met your Mom

*and Gene Krupa played those drums
till three in the morning.*

He doesn't ask about
the CT scan; I don't say.

*Krupa, the way
he beat out those heartbeats.*

Overheard on the F Train

My iPod snatched from an unzipped purse,
I'm left to listen, overexposed
to snatches of dialogue unrehearsed.

Ripped from my private universe,
of Dylan, Marley, Billy Joel
when my iPod's snatched from an unzipped purse.

*"Haven't you heard, Karl's cancer's worse,
melanoma misdiagnosed."*
Snatches of dialogue unrehearsed.

*"Leah just lost her job as a nurse
and her crazy ex-husband's out on parole"*
now my iPod's snatched from an unzipped purse

"My daughter's pregnant with her fourth.
You'd think she'd never heard of birth control."
Snatches of dialogue unrehearsed.

A random act, what appeared a curse,
scattered totems of lives unposed.
My iPod snatched from an unzipped purse.
Gift of snatches of dialogue unrehearsed.

Back and Forth

Dad hurled words across the table at Frank
and me, empty hollow volleys. We'd toss back
streptococcus or *carnivorous*.

Little by little, I quit relying on words, chose
near-silence instead. Syllables jagged crystals
spit from my mouth. Starts and stops

like stutterers' struggles to let loose sounds.
Still I'm tongue-tied, weighing each word
for heft, holding each up to the light.

No wonder my work now is shaping *baba*
and *mima* into words, smoothing a child's stutter,
releasing the "gorilla voice" in a boy who only whispers.

I strain to hear my own still voice beside
the black-ring doves calling back and forth
from the cottonwoods along the river.

After

I used to talk real good. I used
to tell the best stories, the funniest jokes.
But now. I'm shut down, trapped
in my own head. Since the stroke,

I know what I want to say but words
get tangled and twisted all up. I think
"coyote" and "crocus" comes out.
"Excited" turns into "extinct."

My friends don't have time to wait for me
to spit out words. They keep filling in
empty spaces. Half the time, I'd rather
just be by myself—rocking and thinking,

rocking and thinking. I'm a man of Babel,
punished for my pride. Unravelled.

Susan F. Glassmeyer

Hercules Visits My Kitchen

Tonight, waiting for scones to rise in the oven,
the scent of warming yeast and cream
filling the room, I sit down at the table
and flip open the new *Audubon* to learn:

Carrion beetles
using organs of smell in their antennae
can locate a mouse within an hour of its death
and from as far away as two miles.
After flying to the carcass, they drop
to the ground, crash through the litter,
burrow under the body, and by heft
of their magnificent orange backs
lift the mouse remains like mini sons of Zeus,
flip and roll it several feet to a final resting place
where the beetles bulldoze the dirt
and bury the mouse deep under the soil.
(This, all done at night to prevent
rival flies from laying their eggs.) The beetles
then strip the mouse of its fur, covering
the carrion ball with a jelly-like goo,
a refuge of food for their own larvae
to feed upon.

There's more I haven't told you
but the oven timer is ringing
so I must grab my spatula to flip the hot scones
into a pine grass basket to cool . . . breakfast
fuel for my family rising hungry at dawn.

Seeing Movement

For small creatures such as we, the vastness is bearable only through love. — Carl Sagan

In his workshirt dark from sweat
the gardener lays down his hedger
to kneel gingerly in thick ivy.

With the hands of Kuan Yin
he flutters the damaged bird up
to his chest, whispering to it.

While Holding a Shivering Toad in My Hands

I thought about last night's mouse
rattling inside the live trap
in the kitchen drawer.

I can't bring myself to kill
mice anymore. Tried it once
in Michigan. The cottage, quiet
as a book when the snap trap
sprung along the baseboard.
That contraption flew into the air
like a deranged bird pinching in half
the stunned mouse who only wanted
a dumb piece of cheese.

I thought only women standing on chairs
in cartoons screamed at mice
running along the floor.
I did not know a mouse would squeal
when it died like that. I did not know
I would scream.

First Moon of a Blue Moon Month

Tonight while she's asleep
come through the kitchen window above the stove.

Follow the path of her belongings.

Climb the stairs
without making them creak.

Enter the room of her refuge.
Here she has tumbled with night into bed.

Hover awhile.
Let your roundness shimmer above her own.

Be a chandelier to her longings.

Study her lips,
two languages for truth in her sleep.

If you slip under the covers without waking her,
she will lean into you until you are full again.

She can never be touched too lightly.

Parting Word

An attendant props you up, cheerfully
rolls you to a table for a last meal.
Doesn't that look good, sweetheart?

It doesn't. I offer roses and a bag
of dark kisses though we both know
they don't make sense anymore.

What took you so long, you ask, squinting
at me through your good eye. I hold up
your head in the hammock of my hand.

Quiet resumes. No mention of love. You
ask is my other hand on your leg? *Yes.*

Melissa Tyndall

For Our Children, Not Yet Born,
I Preserve the Images of Animals

They are nearly gone: the black-footed ferret,
gloved and bandit-masked, last leopards
fading into Russia's northern forests. You'll never

see a nighthawk's forked plumes and gaping mouth,
watch the Dusky Darter swim Tennessee creek beds,
hear the jumping meadow mouse chirp or its tail

drum against the earth. One night, the woods will empty,
the howl of the red wolf forgotten like a sudden storm—
a strong wind that wails briefly, then dies

in the dark. Here once were 600-pound cats,
fanged and orange as cinders,
and foxes—yes, Fox, your last name—

with wide noses, rufous-colored ears,
and long, black-tipped tails. I hold
them here, until you arrive.

Postcards from the Amer River

A trip to Alaska prompted the first—
backed with near-blue landscapes,
silver-tipped ice whorls, concentric shells.

Last summer, your script spilled past
lined margins, threatened the spiny
bones of sea animals, birds in watercolor,

beachfront sunsets brushed in gold,
lavender and dusty pinks, trapped
the way icebergs entomb volcanic

fragments, carry it for years, before
the black rock ripples, peeling back snow,
upheaving it into crags along the water

the local paper described as God-sized
snowmen melting. At Christmas,
your letters come thrust against Dutch

postmarks. You write of beer and spiced
black teas ripe with honey and cinnamon
and bayberries; how climate or distance

can reframe a place, remove doglocks,
allow migration. Words rise in waves
like relief-maps, from this new country,

set us adrift in reverse, cotton us to memory.
At the first hint of spring, the grass will green
again, grow back into itself, shake off the frost

and black smut whips. In Tennessee,
green foxtails, wild and weedy,
will shatter and scatter their seeds,

and I'll feel the need to write to
you, but there's nothing I want to say.

Haptics

Scientists say we never truly touch—
despite any sensation we might feel,
our electrons begin to push away
the moment we move toward each other.
This is the unquestionable nature
of our universe and its elements,
and we're no more than a collection of
atoms encased by an invisible
force field that allows us to overlap
temporarily, but repels those who
venture too close. It absorbs the shock of
others, protects us from risk. Science claims
contact is just an illusion caused when
our energies brush against each other.
They argue touch is no more existent
than a memory of you—how blue your
eyes look in the dark, the way your long,
dark hair falls into your face when you lean
over the neck of my guitar. No more real than
morning after bruises, evidence of teeth
on my breasts, hands on my throat—than
the recollection of the first time we met.
You cross the room, talk about the summer
storm that rages for hours. You smile. Then,
a low rumble of thunder, a hot vein
of lightning, the rain like a high hat beat
just on the other side of the window.

Film Studies

Ever the Southern gentleman
in your indie film,
you ask before kissing her
on the front porch.
I wonder, if we kissed,
if you'd do it this way
off-screen. Later, you lift
her onto the sink of a hotel
bathroom, your hands running up
her thighs and under her skirt.
I imagine myself in her place—
countertop to pantyhose off,
in one of two double beds, wonder
if your face would look as it did
when you said you loved her.
But the first time you lean in
is during a lull in conversation
on the deck of an East Nashville
bar, the string of lights twinkling,
the fans humming, spinning
like a film reel. I find myself wishing,
not for the crescendo of night sounds,
or our flash forward, but for a loop
of this instant, for the infinite
playback—to preserve the still
moment no movie can capture.

Aubade

After the separation, the first man
to sleep in my bed does just that—sleeps,
fills the vacant side. His long, blonde hair, even
longer than mine, spills across the pillow,
fine as cornsilk strands. Our bodies mirror
each other, hearts flailing against our ribs.
During the night, he pulls my arm over
his torso, grips my thigh to draw my leg
between his, presses my front to his back.
When he shifts, a tribal tattoo licks past
the collar of his white T-shirt and up
his neck. I know the ink runs the other
way, too, almost dips into his waistband,
and it conjures up the memory of him
peeling a shirt over his broad shoulders—
how, after a party, he pushed me down
gently, pinned me back-flat on the carpet.
How he laid on top of me, grew harder
when we kissed, and he fisted the fabric
of my shorts when those kisses dipped
under my shirt, his hair grazing my flesh—
but we stop ourselves.

He wants to pursue
friendship only, he claims, but that's undone
each time our eyes meet across the bartop
and he refuses to look away, nights
we lean against each other on the couch,
our fingers interlaced. Is this what friends
do? He walks the apartment and cleans up
bottles, empty glasses, locks the front door,
turns off any forgotten lights. I lift
up the corner of my blanket for him,
an invitation he accepts
when he climbs in without a word.

Micah Chatterton

Medicine

for Sylvia and her mother

For a nosebleed: drop
something cold, a coin or key,
the length of your back.

Wicked lumbago
needs brown paper ironed hot,
pressed into the small.

To improve eyesight,
pierce your ears and get some gold.
Silver does nothing.

Rheumatism: carry
a young spud in your pocket.
Or soak in Epsom.

Sore throat: tie a wool
stocking round your neck; Father's
sweaty sock will do.

Linseed, lime for burns.
Boiled onion poultice for ears.
Bread poultice for boils.

Bluebag for bee stings.
Warm cow dung for carbuncle,
or draw the devil

out with a hot glass.
Rub butter on a bumped head,
fig leaf on a bruise.

In case of a cut,
a little whiskey leeches rust.
It's good to let dogs

lick an open wound,
but only those you know well,
not some thin-boned stray.

Next, to clot the cut,
use cobwebs, fresh cigar ash—
in a pinch, sugar.

Egg water causes warts,
and touching toads. Spin horsehair
around your finger,

or daub with sow thistle.
If that cure fails, steal a piece
of meat. Rub the wart

into the cold chop.
Bury it in the garden.
Tell no one. The flesh

and the wart decay
together. Some say you need
a dead cat. Jabber—

any meat will do.
No, what we make we make in
in burial, in hiding.

Kin

Remember this, then.
There is a girl at the edge
of town, window jimmied, slipping
lumps of scrambled egg and hard toast
out onto the damp side of the sill.

Morning fog's bitten off all
but the nearest branches of the family
sycamore, and the family of crows
living there, chittering, churning
the clouds with their wings.

There's a line of objects laid neatly
along the dry side of the windowsill:
a pebble, a paper clip, can tabs, beachglass,
earrings, buttons, a cat's broken femur,
the silver half of a heart.

She waits with her nosetip cold
to the pane, quietly breathing herself
into the swirl of an old man's beard,
until one by one, dewhooded
and coin-eyed, the crows come

clutching gifts, offering trade.

A Love Poem

What did you see in there? you asked later,
mermaid red hair floating past my pillow.
I saw the way we leaned to kiss, how we
made cairns of our cold feet, spun up shivers
from still places in our bodies, then fell asleep.
Queen of noses, Vitruvian wife, worried
nursemaid to the world's most delicate dog,
remembrist of first things, spontaneous
cupcake baker, teacher of small children,
teacher of just one unforgotten child—
I thought, *What a mother you'll make, Jenny.*

I saw too how your fear would ache into
panic, beebuzzed by unchecked burners, un-
pulled doors, always waiting for a beltfall,
some fate you might, you should have seen coming:
scuffed heels, uncoastered cups, germs or burglars.
So many days you sat in the driveway,
eyes shaking, willing yourself: Turn the key.

Yet, somehow, you loved me enough to risk
my inevitable tremors of grieving.
Somehow, hours ago, weeks pregnant, you leapt
into the shower fully clothed, new shoes
sopping, mascara bruising the porcelain,
to catch me, collapsed by a memory.

I saw you, the mother you've always been,
the family I never thought I'd have again.

Dropped Tanka

We all learn one day:
something dropped is something lost.
"Out of reach" means "gone
forever," bits of childhood locked
in a mirror of pond water.

He watches my mouth, *lost,*
lost, thrusts against the railing
reaching for the spot
of the splash where the tiger
was thrown, dove, and disappeared.

Once below, all sound
stops. The plastic tiger sinks,
watching a boy cry
by skyfuls its wavering life,
its eternal inch of silt.

Emily Graf

Toolbox

I've had broken teeth dreams
and woke tasting my gums for blood.

A girl said she needed my incisors for art,
pliers shining in her hand.

She was beautiful in the way of people who know
they look good while concentrating.

Fingers stained burnt sienna
and black, she drugged me with whiffs of turpentine.
Surrender slipped gauzy under my tongue.
Of such dreams, Freud says, *anxiety about sexual experience*.
Jung says, *renewal*. Not violence,

but yes,
disorder.

In the dark afterwards, my teeth
were whole. I looked at the blue sliver

of floodlight along the curtain
and knew my life.

Photograph of Two Girls Outside Crazy Horse, South Dakota (2007)

I remember saying, *bury me*,
South Dakota Badlands,
crumbling crowns of black stone and basalt
in the empty ocean of the Midwest.

Under my hand a grasshopper scythed
its butcher paper wings.

We pointed our camera at a motorcycle gang, behind them
a heaving forever of sunflowers,
a harmonica,
the yellow sound of mosquitos.

Or maybe you pointed the camera, and I
held up the unfinished nose of the Indian head.

Bury me, or cut me open.

I was too young to love a landscape so greenless,
too young to think my bookishness was anything but
a free pass to hop from coast to coast
and skip the breadbasket in between.

Years later, bowing
against Chicago's lusty sleet,
I think of you with an imaginary scalpel in your hand,
back of your dad's RV, working on what you believed to be

an improvement of my body,
stunning revision,
while the sun thundered against the plastic curtain
of our small window.

2AM Instagram of Lunar Eclipse

Green sunslant across the dresser should be,
is not quite, an antidote for this hangover. Urgent, the phone

opens its single rectangular eyelid. A few sentences
from you, and I'm drunk again. In the night you scrolled through

the pixelated good times and lit on
my white blouse, my rose moon. How well these images
unscrew your silence. Etched in blue,

you ask for more sweet, you ask if I remember
that we have decided to forget certain unerasable errors.

Taking your words outside, a breeze lifts rosemary to my lips, I breathe it toward you loose
in my two hands, and because I am so glad
to have your attention (this sparkler
burning down to its metal stem)

what is there to say next?

Concession: my love's a shaky bubble drooping
from a plastic wand, all swollen gleam and neon rainbows,

resigned to death in the frail grass.

Striking Matches

I.

You are dealing cards on a picnic table, the wood
bruise-hued, seams crusted chalky-white.
Someone jokes "cocaine" because we're high, I say

"it's probably bird shit." We're playing cards
and I'm talking to make sure you hear me. In the game,
you and I are partners. I forget the rules.
Not Hearts. It's not Hearts but we might be losing—

the rain ceased hours ago but the light that burnishes
your hands is still wet.

II.

You are in your apartment learning Spanish from Cuarón films.
Your shirt smells cold,
of struck matches and want. You're using something sharp to tune
    gears that turn
your hands black. In your hands I am

a melting icicle. I'm not going anywhere but I might be
shrinking.

III.

You have an impulse to gather
all the cards to you while they're still dry, still make that busy click
    when shuffled,
but also
to drink the whiskey that's been passed to you. It tastes

like marigolds might.
Hot crowns, dry flares.

I wonder if I've spoken in the last hour. I wonder if instead I've
    been dancing

in the bloom of light tossed from a window,
revolving to rhythm you shuffle— red-
heart black-heart—song of opposites.

IV.

You are leaning against the wall of the Rijksmuseum and it is
    leaning back on you
while you watch the black crowns of trees
swell with birds, then deflate. Icy feet, I just broke a toenail,

black linoleum
jeweled with blood. You just lit a cigarette and the rush has you
in a headlock.

V.

In my sleep I open my mouth and a spider drops in.
I swallow. Transparent threads
suspend me from the ceiling and I kick my legs like a Rockette,
kick my legs like a doe leaping from a freeway,
kick the blankets free.

You hold still on your side of the bed,
your body curled around a vacancy.

VI.

Once I carried my memories lightly
as you carry another person in water
where what looks like work
is actually
floating.

Kate Magill

NOLA, 2006

Rusted bikes clattering
over rutted streets:
only sound this morning
in a city still learning
how to breathe
now that the flood has receded.

This boy I barely know
takes me to a childhood home.
We stand on the sidewalk
saying nothing,
breathing in the lush smell
of puddles and drowned worms.

We're stripping away
the blackmold sheetrock,
exposing studs
we hope are strong enough,
press of bodies
in the small rooms,

smell of sweat
and waterlogged stuff.
Someone has planted
sunflowers out back.
Their big heads gyre west
to watch the sinking sun.

Down on the sand after dark
listening to black waves
and that air-swelling bayou hum:
we are almost children still,
hurtling forward,
verging on something pure.

Morning, Five Ways

1.

Whitebread morning—
give up on daring.
Focus on something
mundane and immediate:
backbone, for example,
or sinew.

2.

Through the open door,
a furnace blast of morning
The dog has shit a chickenbone
still whole.
No goose today,
no golden egg.

3.

You cannot remember,
standing in a potential friend's foyer,
which boots are yours.
Perhaps finding the correct coat
will spark something.

4.

You have not yet opened your eyes.
The fact of being alive
kicks you in the ribs,
threatens to slit you down the middle
and spill your slick ruby innards
all across the slant of light
whose heat sears through your lids.

5.

It is best to wake first
to give yourself the option
of staying in bed and listening
to his roughhewn breaths
or leaving for an open space
where you can hear your own.

Tanka for The New Year

New Year's Eve, and grey:
cloud upon cloud, swollen full
with unfallen rain.
We are already asleep
on the chill white sunless sheets.

LV Winter, 2015

It's not hot yet and already I'm tired,
trying to read Bronk while the baby sleeps,
trying to sort the husk and hulk of words.

The sun is asserting itself again,
hot butter glow cowing the short grey days,
filling the air with creosote and sage.

Lizard skitter and hummingbird pulses,
the rest is stillness, that desert restraint,
knowing always when and when not to move.

Coffee is blacker in the old palm's shade,
dry fronds brushing my shoulders, somewhat like
a lover's presence, breathing, imagined,

remembered: that kneejerk covering-up
of unfinished pages, this black-on-blank:
I'm sorry, dear, this is not yours to read.

Michael Fleming

Desire

Bangkok, and even the name reeks of it.
The girls in the girlie bars on Patpong
Road, they know that smell, they sell that smell—shit,
cum, curry, poontang, bodies at play, songs
they know you know, dances they know you know,
the English words on their bikini butts,
twinkling in sequins—*WINK. FOXY. GO-GO.*
The smell of dollars, baht, dong, roasting nuts—
they've known that aroma all their lives, who
the hell doesn't? Really, weren't we all born
knowing that smell? The monks, they know it, too,
silent, single file, first dim light of morning,
bearing their bowls, a little day-old
rice, a bit of fish—want reduced to this.
It still smells of suffering—in the folds
of their robes, that whiff of death, saffron, bliss.

Khao-I-Dang

My britches got bigger the day I met you
in a bamboo room, at a bamboo table,
sizing me up (I didn't have a clue)—
so damn sure of a world that never gave
less than what you demanded or deserved
or just made true. Couple of redheaded brats
like us, in a war zone—where'd we get the nerve
and what gave us the right, rat-a-tat-tat
mai pen lai days, Mekong nights . . . we recognized
refugees as people like us: alive,
moon-eyed, bee-stung but still there in the fight,
in a world that needed us, needed our jive—
Khao-I-Dang did too, back when we were brats,
eating up the last of our baby fat.

    for Miss Lola

Lunch

They plopped him down (as we would later say)
like a big bag of potatoes, right there
on our long bamboo table, just the way
they (different they) plopped down lunch, right where
we were eating lunch, yes, that's how it was,

right in the middle of lunch, rice with rocks
to break our teeth and stir-fried weeds and what
may have been chicken, or dog, and the docs
were there, and the nurses, and all of us but
the interpreters, just us and the buzz

of flies and the distant pop-pop that made
the border so exciting, good for our
stories, and then they burst in with that dead
kid soldier, Khmer Rouge, alive an hour
before, here for autopsy, just because.

The Voice of America

In Thailand, where it's never cold, that one
day was cold, a bleak November day, raw, damp—
fresh misery to heap on sickness, guns
and hunger, madness, mud and fear. The camp
went quiet. Every stitch they had, they wore,
rags on rags. We had no more to give them.
We did have a radio, reception poor—
the Voice of America whispered, trembled
from the world we'd left, where election day
was ending, the polls were closing, Wyoming
clinched it: an old fool, nary a gray
hair on a head untroubled by wisdom,
would preside over perpetual morning
with a smile and thrilling hints of war.

Meeting Mrs Ping

Laughing, forty-two to my twenty-two,
and lovely, still the belle of Phnom Penh
even after college, marriage, kids—then
hell: the war that throttled the city, blew
in on rocket wings, the rumble and pop
closer, every day closer, till the city
fell quiet, faceless boys streamed in, no stopping
them, black clothes, tire sandals, eyes unlit,
jungle boys no bigger than their guns came
from darkness to empty the city, empty
everything, kill everything . . . and then
five years later here you were, tart-tongued,
smiling, sassy, the queen of Khao-I-Dang
Camp, reaching through the wire, to me, alone.

for Sunly

Richard Parisio

On a Photograph Taken in Newark, 1929

I imagine he was bored. His job, taking pictures
of auto wrecks for an insurance firm.

He paused a moment here, let vision
of the row of buildings blur in the nimbus

of his cigarette. When it cleared
the alley between tenements

blocked by a slumped fence caught his eye.
Someone wanting in or out had pushed or pulled

then tramped the wooden pickets down.
The fence bears plastered-on advertisements

for entertainments, modern products pitched
to the idle or the curious passerby.

No soul in sight, a thought flashed
in the black box of his head: before

I built a fence . . . He set up his tripod,
fixed the vanquished barrier in his view,

pickets splayed like whales' ribs on a beach,
the soot-dark alley brooding like the sea.

He held his breath and flung the shutter open:
the flash he made was lightning with no rain.

Before his shrouded face the scene
came into sudden focus and the secret

coded in these appearances
fossilized upon a copper plate.

Brown Creeper

Below the plate glass ramparts,
on the simple sidewalk, no tree near,
lay a mouse-sized clump of feathers.
Out-of-context bird, what whispered word
for *forest* brought you here? What lust
for space enticed you past your borders
into this mirror of the sky. You crashed
into our reality, you paragon of drab,
you match for bark and shadows.
I lift you by your spiked tail feathers,
good for hitching up trunks,
admire your bill's curve, perfect
for probing crevices for spiders—
what else could you expect here in this city
but sudden death? For an exile
like you, brown alien, mesmerized
by mere reflection, where is real?
What refuge from sun-dazzle,
tumult, glass, and steel?

I bear you through these Newark streets
till I can lay you in a concrete
urn with pansies. Forget the crude
jest of a citizen of this rough place
hollered as we passed: "Who's got
two slices of bread for that?"
Best melt into the soil of this planter,
dream your way back to leaf-
filtered light. Your body, intact,
pressed into the day, has made a shell
to tilt up to my ear: I listen
past the city's screaming haste to hear
your lilt, your forest song.

Mentor

Outside my morning window spills a wren's
song, like a waterfall. No—effervescent—
like a spring that bubbles
from an unseen source.

Maybe I never really heard till Art King,
understated, most unwrenlike man,
pointed in the song's direction, touched
a finger to his ear before he named the singer.

So many others, more accomplished:
orioles, tanagers, grosbeaks, and of course
the thrush—we first heard, then tried sighting
like augurers, scanning treetops for a sign.

Ready to retire Art King knew each bird
by its song, but hearing failed him in the upper
ranges: one of us young teachers, when we touched
an ear and pointed, might just get a shrug

from Art in answer. One such impossible note
he might or might not hear belonged to the tiny
Blackburnian warbler Art King called "the firethroat."
The bird glimpsed was a match struck

in the leaves, a shock of orange flame
that blazes in the brain's deep folds
four decades later. After those walks we each
went off to teach our classes—but enkindled,

as though we cupped a secret candle
against the wind all day. This morning
I salute the plain brown wren, though I can't see him
answer with a tail flick from his thicket.

Triumphal

Master of nonchalance, the mockingbird
now stays through our northern winters

as if to say, we have entered the new
dispensation, the age of extremes,

when even this endless winter
bears the seeds of endless summer

like acorns under the snowdrifts.
The mockingbird goes for suet,

Leaves sunflower seeds to yankees, pine
siskins flashing sun-yellow from streaked wings.

The mockingbird's hollow bones remember
the sultry south, where Spanish moss

beards the live oaks. He pours the honey
of his song into thick air, milk of moonlight.

Silent today, he bides his time,
can afford to, for the altered world

suits him fine: never mind those icy
blasts, it's clear how things are going.

He's been assigned to call out creatures
in endless mimicry, a roll call of the vanishing.,

The rests in his rollicking aria attest
to the mostly silent: tortoises, polar bears.

Growing up in the city's outskirts I recall
his nonstop tour-de-force on summer nights.

Our bird-loving father feared the wrath
of neighbors kept awake might stop his mouth.

Fat chance. From his rooftop aerial pulpit
the revivalist preacher in his long gray coat

sang out and declared his own redemption:
*here I am, here I am, singing, singing,
whose world, whose world, whose world*

is it now?

The Honey Seeker

La Araña Caves, Spain

Sheathed in mesh mask, white suit, gloves, even high white
rubber boots, I kindled dry leaves and sumac berries to a smoldering
burn in the smoker. Working the bellows, I pumped gray
clouds of smoke around the hive before I dared to lift
a frame away. Mobbed by a posse of bees, I watched their city
with its capped wax cells filled up with slumbering larvae

rouse to repel the siege. I checked for dead or ailing
citizens, signs of mites, found none—left them in the peace
of their amber hoard, their throbbing, multitudinous life.
That day I took no honey, felt no sting, but was a gazer
only, witness to a bounty past my grasping, distilled
from the humming field, the crucible of flowers.

Six millennia have past since I went naked
to scale the limestone cliff to reach this womb.
On the cave wall, in red ochre, see my legs, my long arm
dangling, basket clutched in one hand while the other
plumbs the niche. I am stung and stung but hang on,
reaping, fool and thief and angel. I was chosen.

Jennifer Leigh Stevenson

Honey I'm Headed West

On the night I was born,
my daddy played a gig
at a bar called Cowtown.

So it's right I've got me
a warlike mouth,
a honky-tonk heart.

I'm heaps of trouble, smoke
Benson and Hedges
like a lonesome locomotive,

drink bourbon from a truck
stop coffee cup. My soul's
just some no-tell Motel

with most the neon shot out
of its shivery sign. Or a mirror
that's lost some of its silver.

When we met I told you
I'm a dead end on a dirt road.
But you didn't pay any mind.

This summer stands
as the wettest on record
but nothing's getting green.

June bugs throw themselves
at the bare bulb on my porch,
trying to hump it to oblivion.

Cicadas preach white noise
from blue ash pulpits, but
none of us are wise enough

to hear their truth—
that the world will end
before the evangelists do.

I, too, call and holler
for you, a small town
Siren with an ivy crown.

Load up the truck with all
you can fit, I tell you—
it's time to go. A sparrow

nested in the awning over
your front door, and some
cold-eyed crow'll eat those eggs

one at a time. But hey, you
and me both know: wild
isn't the same thing as free.

Undone

We open on an unmade man
sleeping artful in an unnamed bed.
A gentle ribbon of sunlight
sighs through the blinds
from his shoulder
to his hip
to the sheet
like some kind of ceremonial
sash and sword. He didn't mean
to be here.

A fly buzzes frantic in the window
and the ceiling fan clanks.

We now part the steam
to visit her in the shower.
Over the pedestal sink hangs
a mirrored medicine cabinet
with a slot inside to toss old
razor blades. Her pale skin gleams
cream. She slicks her palms
over her hair, blinks, her wet
eyelashes dark and heavy.

She hums a lonely melody,
one that has fluttered
unfinished at the edges
of her for weeks. She picks
and picks at it and when
it comes to her
it just
opens in her hands.

Last night, his fingers brushing the barest
paisley on her neck, he kissed her jawline
with such cinematic longing that she climbed
onto him and said, *Stop keeping yourself from me.*

The Dangers of Prose, Love

I lick my finger,
flip the page,
"fray to fight
fray to unravel"
so I have some choices.
Either way it all comes apart.

Your work is shining, methodical,
blown glass turned from a molten
thing into tender tiny creatures
that fit in my palm.
I can almost see them breathe.

Not my poems, though.
I want to write
blunt force trauma
with a gauntleted fist,
smashing reckless,
jaw aching with anger,
wrecking everything.

But Baby, I never can conjure
you. Something phrases
should curve around light
and easy: your wicked
mouth, your cinnamon smell.
You rhymed and dined me
and dug in my dark
trying to find me a muse.

I got nothing like that in me.
So I take my forearm, sweep
it across all you ever said before
but it doesn't matter. The sound
of 100,000 crystalline words
shattering
can't cover up the echo
the thrill of your voice

Circe in Business

I wear all black, a high-necked frock,
and a straw hat to thwart the southern sun.

My plants, such lovelies, in rows
taller than I, bow now in summer

breeze. They forget how deadly
they are in their beauty, waxy

berries bright, leaves trembling.
I've made quite a name for myself.

Flowers in high violets, yellows and other
likely hues, (those colors are suspect

those colors are a bruise.) But no
matter. I wear leather gloves,

pinch those flowers and berries
at the base. Apply a little heat to help

the harm along. Women come to see
me when rage vignettes their vision,

walk along my wares, smooth their hands
over the glass bottles and decide just

how he should go. I don't do gentle,
so you won't find any soporifics.

Hemlock, certainly, if you'd like
to watch him gasp, or belladonna

to sink him into a delirium, dilate
his pupils as though he were tumbling

in love again, but by then could
you bear it? Wolfsbane hurts,

as I understand it, stirs up the belly,
sends saliva to froth in his mouth.

I don't need magic anymore
so it's lucky I don't have it.

This, my dear, is true,
for every one of you
who seek me and weep:
Later in your Paris Green parlor

you'll look in the mirror
and see a face tight with triumph,

wild eyes dark and bird-bright.
Mark me. Not more than a drop

to stop his heart. And don't get
caught. Get even.

Quarry

Why do you want to talk now?
I'm barefoot, dusty and bleeding.
I replenish my stones.

I speculated so long in labored silence . . .

When I realized the weight of all these words unsaid,
when the chasm growled between us, filled with cruelty
and doubt I still couldn't shout
and I couldn't scream or say anything true or fraught.

I tossed a rock down into the yawn below
(where our pressure broke the yard),
watched that rock fall and gather pebbles
and momentum and felt bored. You rendered me
irreverent, chained to a shrug and a hum.

You once whispered kindness but
now you are a wooden placard
hanging haphazard over my front door:
"Abandon All Hope Ye Who Enter Here"
burned into the grain.

This morning my back porch opens into this canyon.

It's not powerlessness, or fear, but rather an
unbecoming. Eyes burning across the crisis
until they fade into embers of distance. 'Til
calamity supersedes life and you and me

and we failed to be.
All this earth over our bones.

All that time.

We replenish our stones.

Laurel Eshelman

Tuckpointing

The Virgin Mary up at St. Mary's is wrapped in a drop cloth
the color of stone. It is pulled over her face,
drawn down around shoulders to her feet, the corners seized
and tied in a bunched knot across her waist.
She is mute, visionless in the blankness of sacking, muffled
from sparrow calls in the cedars.
No eye may look upon her.
In a week her son sets his sights
on the city, dashes in with the crowd
and no caution. In two he is
besieged and bared.

March snow weighs Mary's wrappings down
upon her. The shroud sags—
her right hand, pale stone appears,
three fingers raised against shadows.
Her staying power pierces like a sword, the fibers darken
over her breast. Snow splays
across her naked toes—
a white dove
shelters there.

Home Game

A winter rain pounds the roof
like the clamor at a home game
when the basketball is stolen,
dribbled downcourt and launched
on a long smooth arc.
As night gives in and ice lies down
the crowd hushes and awaits the ball's descent—

by midday the siren at the volunteer fire station wails.
The township maintenance guy slides the alley,
mechanics from the garage sprint the highway,
boys we shouted for in the old gym as they set up the play,
lofted the risky three-pointer.

They rev fire trucks to the curve beyond the ridge
while they gear up, readying to ply deliverance.
The memory of feet stomping wooden bleachers
in the stifling gymnasium embraces those shivering
on the shoulder.

—it rushes the hoop
and swishes,
the crowd rises,
their voices hoarse
with praise.

Outpatient

She lies on the table.
They slather her with gel,
slide the ultrasound wand
over every contour line of her breast,
then prod.
She remembers her morning walk,
the dark calves being driven off,
the hot scent of hair and hide
rising off the confined cattle.
It rises from her memory now and permeates
the room.
A needle pierces her breast,
her gown slips off,
the cows bellow and her sweaty fingers
grip the table.

On the drive home,
the hills embroidered gold
with mown and baled hay
prick her eyes.
She hears the calves—
they are bawling now.

You Call Me to Jump

You call me to jump into a pool.
The water is dark. It looks deep.
I do not recognize the place.
Kids swim and flail,
ducklings without instinct,
some drop below the surface.
My day grows short. I hear your voice

and I hear a six-year-old yelling at me—
Auntie, help, I need help.
I push the kindergartener
up the hill on his bike
and listen to his non-stop shouts—
Look, I can ride a bike.

Can I push up my sleeves,
lift my skirt
and jump in?

Here I am,
hitting the cold surface.
Keep calling.
I need to hear your voice.

Barry W. North

The Molotov Cocktail of the Deep South

I swore I would never
lie down with one of your kind,
and it was not even within
flying distance of possible
that I would ever let one of you
relive the slave days at my expense
by taking me from the rear,
although I must admit I had, on occasion,
used my vision of such a coupling
to amuse myself and others
with the image of a
modern-day wannabe aristocrat,
the color and texture of vanilla ice cream,
gone completely soft,
like so many of your tribe
have a tendency to do,
getting his rocks off
by mounting me from the posterior position,
in honor of his long departed heroes.
I pictured him
as a ludicrous caricature of his ancestors,
clad only in rolls of milky flab,
riding me, like one of his prized fillies,
while lashing my rump
with a tiny whip,
to match his annoying little node,
all the way to the finish line,
at which point,
wild-eyed and exuberant,
he raised his hand in victory,
as the Caucasian crowd,
overcome with generational nostalgia,
cheered for the triumphant return of privilege
as it was in the glorious slave and plantation days.

I must confess to you that
my unbridled enjoyment
in depicting of your people's
moral corruption and physical debauchery
showed me how satiric ridicule of my own folk
might seem like great entertainment to certain
twisted members of your bloodline.

Then you,
white as a damn Ku Klux Klan robe,
came along, and
to hear my girlfriends tell it,
ruined everything.
Like a medicine man with a magic elixir,
they say you somehow managed to scramble
my little black circuit board.
They claim I am no longer myself
and with that I cannot argue.
I am so out of whack, at this point,
the only thing I know
is when I look at your face
I am struck colorblind
and at that mysterious
juncture inside my brain,
where animal meets human,
there is a fire raging,
sparking off boiling daydreams
of the two of us making what is still
the Molotov cocktail, here, in the deep South,
with me screaming,
like the fool I so clearly am,
as we burn old Dixie down.

The First Day

> *Today is the first day of the rest of your life...*
> —Charles Dederich, a reformed alcoholic and founder of Synanon.

The day after her
only daughter's suicide,
she came out
of the upstairs bedroom,
dressed in white,
like a virgin bride instead
of a grieving mother
and now childless divorcee.
She hesitated at the top of the stairs,
and then slowly descended,
as though going once again
to unite with her man
and begin their life anew.
In an unexpected vision, she saw
the faces of her deceased parents
floating beneath her, their sparkling eyes
full of hope and love just as
they had been on her wedding day.
She stopped at the foot of the stairs,
stripped off all of her garments,
and trudged forward to the reality
waiting for her in the kitchen.

Inside the doorway, she paused
to take a few deep breaths,
and then started the ordeal.
With sponges, bleach, bucket, and mop
she cleaned the room for hours,
from ceiling to floor,
until, by mid-afternoon, the task was complete.
With her hands raw and bleeding,
she stood on the gleaming ceramic tile,
covered with her teenager's insides,
her skin glistening
like the scales of a fish.

She left the kitchen,
went through the downstairs bedroom,
where her only child had been conceived,
entered the bathroom
and stepped into the shower.
She let the water flow over her
and watched what remained
of her fifteen-year-old daughter
swirl around and get
sucked down the bathtub drain,
at which she continued to stare until
she was looking at her three-year-old,
full of life,
waiting for her bathwater to disappear,
at which point, just like she always used to do,
she suddenly tossed her hip to the side,
flipped her hands out at shoulder height,
glanced up, and said:
"Look, mom, it's all gone."

All That Glitters

The trees at the edge of town
seek in vain to be heard
with every passing wind.
The crescent moon
and stunning array of stars
have not a single disciple
on the empty street,
but inside the pulsating nightclub,
women, wearing neon skirts
and perfume which smells like money,
sit cross-legged on high-backed stools,
sipping cocktails
not worthy of the name,
surrounded by men
whose clothes jingle
like pocket change when they move,
and whose eyes, when reflected
in the dazzling mirror behind the bar,
seem, at times, to flash
inside their heads like some sort of
genetic, next-generation bling
making its ghoulish debut
in the midst of a receptive crowd.

Thanks

Mom,
for the gift of life
because it doesn't take a Nobel Prize Winner
to figure out that without it I would have been,
from the beginning of time
part of the black pall of absolute nothingness,
which, for some strange reason,
has just made Archibald MacLeish's
stunning little work of art
The End of the World pop into my mind,
a gem, it occurs to me, I would never have had
the joy of reading for the first time,
or the pleasure of re-reading over the years
to remind myself that life is a circus
there is no way out of,
even if you try to play it safe
by being only a spectator.

And thanks, Dad,
for the unconditional love,
which I have carried with me
every single day of my seventy years,
like that little pocket knife
you always kept in your trousers
that seemed to be able to do more work
and get you out of more jams
than a truckload of specialty tools.

And thanks, God,
for letting us all die,
often in bizarre, unexpected, and brutal ways,
because without death,
life would just not seem so precious to us.
Funny how that works,
but I guess you would have to have your perspective
to fully appreciate the humor in it.

You Are Also What You Don't Do

When my country went to war based on a lie,
I saw the face of my dear dead father
as he instructed me to always tell the truth.

When my country engaged in torture,
I thought about the astonishing irony
of every talk show host
and every concerned parent in America
condemning, with high moral indignation,
the act of bullying.

When my country said that the euphemism
Enhanced Interrogation Techniques
had produced valuable results,
I wondered how it would be to
live in a world in which everyone believed
the end always justifies the means.

In spite of all that,
when my country violated its principles,
I did not take to the streets to protest.
Instead, I stayed in my comfortable
three bedroom house pretending
it was not being done in my name;
sat at my spacious dining room table,
enjoying the fruits of the land,
as though not a single thing had changed,
as though what was being
done on my property, somehow,
had nothing whatsoever to do with me.

Charles C. Childers

Camouflage

Under the shade of a barren
apple orchard, little children play
at poverty.

With no shoes, they smear dirt
on their noses and clothes.
All innocence in hillbilly blackface.

They make mock depression dolls
with their lunch left-overs, chuck rocks
at beehives, pummel a copperhead corpse
with fiberglass fence-posts and fish for leaves
in mud puddles with bits of string.

They were sensible enough
to bring these things
from the air-conditioned city.

By the time they return
to the farmhouse, they're covered
in burs, like coonhound curs,
new clothes all tattered and torn.

Their aged grandma catches them,
and tans their backs with a switch.
The children, tear-choked,
scream incoherently
at the injustice of it all.

Privilege

It was a generation that crept
along on knee-pads.
These, the picayune people,
preyed upon
the Almighty Dollar,
panhandling in cashmere suits
and charmeuse silk dresses.

Recessive

My mother's in the living room,
staining the walls, spraying
them with the sickly sweet yellow
smell of cigarillo smoke,
using calloused hands as an ashtray,

and my father's out of work.
I can hear him in the bedroom
suppressing sobs,
like smothering puppies,
into a bed-wallowed pillow.

They barely speak between
their gasping, both fighting for air
in their claustrophobic closeness.

Underseam

Between the incessant barking of the mixed-
pomeranian pup and the cutting clink
of knives on plates, nothing was audible—
a silence intolerable.

Of course, not racist, they kept their traps
shut. But still, she was a stain on the white tablecloth,
which one hides on the underside
or else attacks vigorously with bleach.

Synchronized

It's dusk, and fireflies dot
the horizon in every direction,
communicating with their own kind
of Morse code. Brief dashes and dots
lighting up the trees, signals intermingling
with the indecipherable effects
of this midsummer evening.

As I fiddle with my notebook, trying
to capture the intricacies
of their language, I realize
its a frequency which has been denied me,
the antenna of my linguistic ear
broken to the complex cries
of their community.

One of theirs lands on my hand
in an act of sheer defiance,
as if to further my frustration
flaunt its semantic prowess,
and began to brandish
a rather aureate display
in order to irritate me.

. . . ‒ ‒ . . .

I smashed it and felt satisfied,
demonstrating my own form
of intellectual supremacy.

Ricky Ray

Listening

A man, tired after a day's long journey, comes to a cabin in the woods and opens the door. The hinges squeak and the sound of wings shuffles overhead. He walks in, waits for his eyes to grow into the darkness, to make out its forms.

He finds a stool by a table and sits to rest, not wanting to try his back on the floor. He has no sleeping bag and does not feel like piling leaves. He puts his head to the table and listens.

It speaks through his skin, his mind, tells him all he can remember of tables, of wood, trees, seeds and growth, of splinters, termites, rotting and soil.

Eventually his mind takes him to the edge of the field where he grows quiet and humble, where his inner voice no longer speaks for the table, and feeling takes over.

He sits there a long time, until his forehead begins to hurt. Then he lifts his arm and runs his hand along the edge of the table, slowing to finger its nicks, its rough spots, stopping at the rounded corner.

There, in the oily smoothness that might be the inner elbow of someone he once caressed in the night, he grasps the part of the table, the part of the tree, the part of himself that, then as now, he does not and cannot know.

In that shadow of time, in the descending darkness he belongs to the cabin and falls asleep, waking when his neck grows hot under the morning sun. If he dreamt, he doesn't remember.

He listens, not to the table this time, but to the living day— the things he can hear, and the things he can't. The hinges squeak. His stomach grumbles. A box of crackers, quiet as a skeleton, stales in a hidden alcove behind the cupboard. A small-breasted birdsong slips under the door.

The Crossroads a Pound of Flesh Is

Sun and water become seed and soil
become timothy and clover
sharp and soft in the evening,
lips wet, fuzzy with milk, manure in the barn,
calves the color of gloves and coal
grazing in the rain.   Add years and slaughter:
a block of meat bought from a beef farmer,
blue-green plaid kilt,
splashes of red in his beard, slight New England
twang, an upturn at the corner of his mouth,
neither smile nor smirk, etched, when
he needs to put it on.   Add minutes and sweat:
this block, ten dollars, marbled with fat,
frozen pound in plastic pressed between palms,
freezes the hands I wrap around my dog's Irish ears
as we sit on the bench, inching back from the sun,
gently rocking in the rise and fall of her breath
as she raises her nose to study
a scent I cannot detect,
folds upper lip under lower canine,
pensive about its statement.   Add seconds and sense:
come to some conclusion, she crosses one paw
over the other, tufts of cinnamon pluming
between toes, drops her jaw, unrolls
her tongue, lets drip one bead
of saliva and pants the heat away.

Quiet, Grit, Glory

Sometimes I go silent, not intending to,
just following an inclination to be quiet,
and then some shadow will pass
and I'll think to respond, engage again,
throw voice and opinion,
take the counterpunches they ignite,
but before I do I turn my head aside
and hear the woods calling,
and the pull of that call tugs deeper,
so I go into the woods,
and when I come out to some
road or town or intent to be social,
I feel obliged to live up to the weight
the silence has spread over us,
and I can't, the word weighs too much,
puts a whole world of gravity in the tongue,
so I stay silent—I sit with it until it breaks.

And sometimes that breaking is heavy,
the shattering of metal, lead, hammers,
brick you have to chew until
the teeth work it down to grit,
then the tongue resumes its fighting shape of yore
and lashes like I've always been in the ring,
even when I left all buildings
and said nothing but what was said
by the ring of the horizon.

And sometimes that breaking is light,
a feather let loose in leaves,
the day's simple rituals—
telling how something tastes,
how the bones have felt their marrow—
sometimes a curtain blows aside
and the good of conversation announces itself
like the good of morning
in unachievable, everyday glory.

Sometimes the lips part, the wind of the woods
rises from the lungs, the tongue begins
its dance against the teeth and,
with one person in the presence of another,
the truth—long-stirring, time-sifted—
finds the mouth parched and prepared to speak it.

A Way to Work

I

Good morning.

A body is not just one body.
I inspect every part I can, touch parts that rarely get touched.

I feel the aliveness of being on both sides of the touching: toucher
 and touched.
I can't depend on this to continue, but I do.

This body will fail me, and when it does, I won't mind, I think.
Whether mind or mine or I survive the body: shuts me up.

It opens me at the same time, parts the air as if somewhere in the
 back of my eyes, I could turn on another frequency of vision and
 see the insides of being.

As if seeing the insides of being weren't what we're doing, us
 innards.

II

Now the cells constrict, the blood slows, the skin screams against
 going numb.
It is really fucking cold. Brr doesn't begin to describe it.

Breath crystalizes on my glasses. It hurts to wipe them off.
I remove them and thread their arm through a hole in my lapel.

Hello, blurry world.
Dogshit, I can still see you coming for my shoe.

III

There is attention and there are kinds.
The weather has a hand in it: twenty, a hundred and four, fifty
 below.

The blessed seventies, before heatstroke, before dementia?
I have thirty-some years to find out. What an assumption, the
    future.

IV

Desire is the greatest liar I know.
It even gives us the want to believe in its visions. Says *see, you
    want this*. And we do.

It will be warm when I get home.
There will be water in the pot and the stove will work and the tea
    will raise my core temperature.

I will sip it thinking of my wife's soup and eat her soup letting my
    thoughts dissolve in flavor.
She will ask me how I like it and I will have to think to tell her.

She will question the level of salt.

V

I arrive at work. The office is cold. There is no stove. My
    colleagues say hello.
We generate warmth for one another because this is our chosen
    family.

We will either choose or be forced to leave it.
If death is the force, and gravity's here, the ground will take us
    back.

I mean the force that makes us leave each other could be the end of
    earth, in which case gravity may not matter, the ground may not
    be under.

VI

My mother wants her and her mother's ashes blown from the tops
    of the Cherokee mountains.
I hope when I get to the top the cold doesn't drive me down.

I'd like to watch where the ashes go.
I'd like to live long enough to offer them to the wind, intact
    enough to climb.

I imagine them blowing back on me, sleeping up there,
    waking up sore and comfortably dirty.
The kind of dirty one can never wash clean. The kind of
    dirty one wouldn't want to.

The kind of dirty that becomes the residue of family lore,
    whether that family is one's bloodline, one's loveline, or
    the line of sentient being.

Or the line of being, sentient or not.

Poems That Are Poems Even Though They Aren't Poems, I Swear It

A poem doesn't have to be etched on the page,
warm in the mouth or caught in language;
it can be unspoken in the course of your day,
it can be *the* unspoken course of your days;
it can be the way you conduct attention,
emotion, the way you treat someone,
the way you turn toward an echo down an alley
that sounds like some long-sought call
from another version of your soul;
it can be your heart as it lifts almost
out of your chest in response,
your voice as it strikes your throat
as an organ of the body
and an organ of the earth;
it can be work, streaks of pain,
the undetectable merger of days,
rust-heeled nails, unanswered mail,
wild strawberries in the mouths of cats;
it can be the way you look at
the light, the light filtering dust
and all that comes to dust
onto your window
and down to its ledge,
the black granite ledge shining,
the stormgates of your pupils shining;
it can be the way you reach out your hand
to wipe away the dust
and wonder how it all comes to this.

Cassandra Sanborn

Bird Watching

See, I want to tell you about the crumbs on the windowsill—
or are they coffee grounds,
dark and small,
smearing against the fake wood?

—well, it doesn't matter.
(You will say it never matters,
before you sigh,
tap one long finger against your glasses.)

I only want to explain:
our window isn't
clean anymore.

But this is where we saw the birds
suddenly burst together from that tree,
the one with all the red berries
flinging themselves into the air

as if driven by some foe I could not see
as if the ground would melt their claws
or as if the dirt would cling to their feathers,
pull them beneath the grass.

I said *I would
never want to be a bird*
and you asked
why I wanted to live with my feet on the ground.

One bird fell from the group,
dropped straight down
onto the grass.

I said something about always wanting
a door to close.

You put your hand on my shoulder,
tangled cold fingers into my hair.

The fallen bird's wing
bent behind her back.
I turned to answer you,
lost her in the grass.
Do you sit there on Sundays now,
while I am away trying to remember
how to love?
Do you eat your pancakes
and watch for her?

I had forgotten her slow hop,
the way she stayed behind.
Or perhaps they left her,
brown feathers half-hidden in green grass.

Last Night

Maybe the world began like this:
a hand,
palm up in the bottom of the basement
a quick gesture to the open window,

where arborvitae roots crawl through the screen
as if we have been hiding
better ground inside,
as if we know how to help them grow.

Three of us, awake,
and someone says something about isolation,
surviving the apocalypse
or roaming the stars.

Either way, all of us separated
from the world by that screen,
set apart from everyone sleeping above,
those left outside.

I lean back on the couch—
purple, overstuffed.
Gilded graduation announcements on the table,
gold against the dark wood.

Say *I think it's all because we want to be alone*

us and the quiet of the basement:
the muted television,
the roots just tapping,
that vein of water creeping down the wall.

And Julie waves her hand again,
says *if we're pretending*
let's imagine it's only space.

(We want our families to be alive,
staring up at the sky, imagining

we are that light *no that one*
waiting—we might return.)
Ellie maps out our ship,
blue ink on notebook paper,
five buildings united in air, five people in each.
Tell me who you would take.

Who do you take
when the universe is sprawled at your feet,
when launching means everyone else will just keep living,
lives spreading out below like roots in good dirt.

Ellie's pen hovers over pale blue lines;
a breeze brushes my neck.
The roots in the window tremble.

Botany Lessons

On the radio, the man who can hold a note
longer than I can hold a breath
sings about fields in Indiana
and hickory trees.

His voice wobbles.

I have lived by his fields
and never seen a hickory.

Unless I did—
unless I, careless,
saw one, all rough bark
(complicated leaves)
and called it an ash,
wondered how it survived those bugs.

My mother's grandmother would have known.

See, once she took the shotgun
from the closet in the laundry room,
propped it on her shoulder,
tried to kill a vulture
sitting on the fence in the shade.

See, he was looking
like he knew something
and goddamn those were her trees,
her walnuts rotting in the grass,
her birds hiding in the leaves.

Older

When I get my letter from the graduate school,
my mother tells me about ink on her fingers
and typewriter tape,
stacks of papers crammed into corners,
retreats under golden, crumbling sycamore leaves.
Whispering to almostbrown grass:
The Star. The Post!

She puts her hands on my arm,
says, but I got all of you.
Her cold fingers—
how's that for an inheritance?—
tighten, then release,
move up to stroke my hair.

A callus catches;
I wait for her to untangle the strands.
Of course I'd never give you up.
She frees them without looking,
her eyes on my letter.
My hair falls against my neck.

Revelation

There is no carpet in the office,
just cool, green tile
so she slips off her shoes,
presses her toes against the ground,
lets the heat from her body slip
into fading linoleum.
She reads the financial report to me,
shakes her hair.
Curls bounce in the air

and I look at her shoes—
black leather, shiny,
but worn by the heel.
She has discarded them
like we would discard water bottles at the beach:
empty for a moment
until you need it again.

And for a moment I want to say
I just finally understood prayer—
but that's another lie.

Maybe it's only the kind of prayer
I knew when I was a girl:
hands clasped
like I was holding on to something,
reciting the names of the people I loved
until my father turned out my light,

and I, left in the dark,
let the words stop dripping off my lips.
Left them lying there,
a pile by my side,
waiting until morning.

Linda Sonia Miller

Eclipse

Last night, front lawn, the Dad stands
after arriving late from work at the E.R.
where he's watched a thirteen year old girl
slip into a coma—and puts his arm
around the shoulders of his 12 year old
daughter, now as tall as he.

They stare into that starlit velvet dome
eyes on the moon slowly enveloped by earth's
shadow, its fullness diminished, then enhanced
as it turns rusty brown then iridescent red
each shade, each change mysterious
the way earth's perfect roundness eclipses

the moon's until it vanishes
beneath this planet's exact otherness
as though moon and earth were twins
or friends sharing a moment
as parent and daughter might share
some unspoken understanding perhaps

on a night like this, she still child enough
to love his company best, he still energized
after a long, tiring day by the presence
of his sylph-like daughter, who asked him
to wake her, hours past her bedtime, to witness
this transformation together.

Kaida Does The Stomp

"A wise man will make more opportunities than he finds."
—Sir Francis Bacon

Gray autumn day, sliver of sun, tennis court bestrewn:
leaves, puddles, abandoned toys. Playground bereft
of children but for the two-foot tall, fairy/elfin creature
in blue corduroy coat embroidered with flowers and owl,
feet in three-inch slippers, pink leather petals on each set of toes
—barely anchored to earth.

She pauses at a puddle, studies a floating spire, yellow trees
grizzled trunks, rhythmically stomps each small foot in turn,
ripples, unravels the scene, runs to the next puddle, pauses
stares, stomps again, a dance of sorts, puddle to puddle
across the court, oblivious of all but the mystery of a world
afloat, sound, feel of water splashing

until she reaches the net, raises that shabby curtain,
stagehand and star, crawls beneath, faces her audience
of one—and applauds herself.

Full Circle

(after the painting by Peter McCaffrey)

On new legs she stands, eyes wide
afraid—it's the world after
that moist landscape, unremembered
mostly lost

before that other
muddled affair, kaleidoscopic
dark and bright
slowly coming into focus,

Timid, legs placed wide
for traction in this unfamiliar place
she glances back
and bleats

newly sprung from one unknown
to another, and much later
another still awaits her
but this time perhaps

she'll be brave, replete
sweet hay, sun-drenched grassy plain
strong bovine body, calves of her own
that kept her warm.

Delivery

I stretch into the pose: inhale, exhale
bend, stretch
                         feel body and mind
                         attempt escape

morning news: six year old boy, hand broken
by his father's torturer
                         two-thousand refugees trapped
                         in no-man's land

my joints fight September's chill
a phone call:
                         my mother tells me she cannot see
                         only blurs and memories

across the room, rope of sunlight
a bird appears, flutters
                         against the windowpane
                         as if trying to break in

disappears, re-appears from that blue-gold
high above the green
                         soars to a neighbor's roof, a sign
                         above his side-door: *Deliveries*

descends, looks in at me again—beak and black-seed eyes
press against the pane
                         as if my small, constructed world
                         clapboard walls built long ago

promise permanence or safety, while I desire that vast blue
clouds wild, buoy of light:
                         ascend, descend, gold to green
                         and back again—*Deliver Us* I read

The Weight of Birds

(after the painting by Peter McCaffrey)

Even the soul
    though beautiful
        and weightless
            is not free

except perhaps
    in the warm womb
        newly hatched
            into otherness

but even then
    tethered
        by that blood-red thread
            to history.

Everything tries
    to hold us
        though we emerge
            complete

cut adrift
    most ourselves
        asleep or alone
            in perfect stillness

as if perched on the shore
    of a pond at dusk
        to find one's self
            submerged

then afloat
    finally
        aloft.

J. Lee Strickland

The Music of the Spheres

Her disappointment makes them strangers.
In her voice he can sense the abyss
his lame attempt at humor cannot bridge.
Conciliating words spawn newer hardness in her jaw.
Her green eyes find another place to stare.
She knows him all too well,
as he knows her.
Galileo to her Bruno he recants
while she insists on burning at the stake.
She's all inscribed in stone to him, the tale
as clear today as when the chisel struck.
Elisions of eroding years are glossed.
Time-softened planes fail of detection.
Recalcitrant remembering recarves
each faded line, each miniscule imperfection.
Inside the stove, the fire rails
against the glass (it would be free).
Outside, frigid air beats on the walls
(it would come in).
None would touch the theme of freedom now.
The one locked in, the other out,
their wheeling flings new mud
from ancient ruts.

High Tide

I found her at the water's edge
kneeling in a patch of gravel.
Her hair had taken on the shape of sleep
and would not let it go.
The Tigris and Euphrates of her arms
joined at her hands,
which held a pile of smooth, clean stones.
Tears streamed down her cheeks.
"They're *so* beautiful," she said.

How To Know The Grasses

Mother knew the grasses.
As I crawled about she'd say to me,
"Don't put that in your mouth,
Sweet thing."
Saving me from certain death.

I knew the grass
 against my butt
beneath a spruce
in darkness with
a girl named Fern
whose husky breath
smelled sweetly
of cheap whiskey.

Now grass seeds shed their chaff
and fill the cheeks
of tiny mice
who know the grass
that fills their nest
will be their sweet salvation
or,
them swept up by hawk or owl,
the seed in spring
will sprout a riotous clump
of sweet lush blades,
a monument to missing mice.

Practice

I'm practicing to be
a sentimental old man.
Already there is practically nothing
that will not bring me to the verge of tears.

I'm practicing with too
much drink,
not to steam with anger,
but to simmer in a maudlin stew
of foggy reminiscence.

I'm practicing to love
my old, drunk, maudlin self,
and not, hating myself,
to be a hater of everything else,
jealous of all that will still be
when I am gone.

Anna's Plague

Tiny bugs come to drink at his eyes while he sleeps.
One or two stop to graze on the salt paths that lead
From his eye, down his cheek, to the cleft of his ear
Before making their way to the well of his tears.
His deep, blinding sorrow, to them, is a fountain,
A treasure of rich, subtle flavors and scents.
They drink after crossing broad wastelands of linen
Unmindful of anguish and tormented dreams.

Sorrow-filled dreams evanesce with the dawn
Though he still feels her hands on his chest when he wakes,
His breathing made hard by that fading dream-touch
And a vaguely sensed movement around his closed eyes.

In the dim light of day's edge he flees to the wood
Where crepuscular songs weave a dirge-like lament.
Such a threnody strung on the darkness within
Is, without, reinforced by the dank, clinging cold.
Spider webs wave like flags in the mouldering straws,
Festooned with the moisture of night's fading damp.
Tattered leaves, like rags, limply flap in the breeze.
One, releasing its grip, sinks to ground.
In the bark of gray trees tiny lenticels wink,
Each a vessica pisces which hints at once-sacred
Geometries prized by the ancients, now lost,
Or the bright eyes of elves in a happier tale.

In his mind swarm ineffable thoughts of the past,
Crowding the images caught by his eye.
Elves become monsters, leaves become blades
Whirling sharp on brown branches like gilt-handled swords.
His legs fold beneath him. He sinks with the leaves.
At the edge of a whispering stream he succumbs
To despair-laden dreams in a sleep of despair,
While bugs vainly search for the eyes that they love.

Erin Dorso

March in Manarola

Water presses and slips
green silk over stone,
a mother's hand over hair,
tangling loose strings of foam, floating
away,
the broken
cat's cradle, the rope
and the rock and the sea,
the sea,
the sky and the rock and the
red boats lined up,
waiting

On the Drive Back to Andersonville

Snowdrifts rush across Lakeview Drive.
Naked tree trunks pull white coats on their backs
heaving polar fur bit by bit
until they rear up, ancient monsters
showing their dark bellies.
Branches, bald and bone,
each limb capped with pearl talon.
Translucent snakes shine off the ends, slicing
wind as we scream by them at 65.

I shiver against the window on the way back out
to the stout, less dignified part of the city
just after New Year's midnight.
From across the console, my husband sighs:

Isn't the snow lovely?

In the Kitchen

Chopping cabbage
the way I taught myself
from eating nabe so many times at the izakaya
around the corner.
No technique—
just hacking at squares of leaf
the best I know how.
We're Italian

and I've watched my mother cut the peppers
wide and firm for cacciatore
lean strings in the salad.
Daikon is probably the same
and I julien an in-between, indecisively sized amount
of about a handful too many

and toss the extra white strips
in my clean, white bin.
My neat kitchen hides the cook
I keep shamed in the cupboard.
I poke and prod at the ordered implements,
order my boyfriend around,

act the woman of the house
while crumbs build up in the dark corners
a real woman would know about
and the nabe leaks bright kimuchi
into cracks in the straw floor.

Fig Keeper

In the evening, I watch the fig garden
below my window.
The air stills.
I wait, listless,
for stretched leather skins to split open
and expose what's been ripening
inside.
Grow a person,
I imagine,
who will speak my tongue,
sweet and pitted and
present.

Holly Lyn Walrath

Behind the Glass

Reproduction, as you put it, is a biological superlative.
Red wine seeped up to our eyeballs
and spilled out on my cheeks
and splashed onto the loud city lights.
Behind our words stood a glass wall
shored up with ego, youth, mud, and sand.
(The ocean breeze tries to tear it up with its teeth
but in summer like a stalwart old sailor
shipwrecked after his last voyage,
his head rimmed with hoarfrost,
clinging to the salt soaked rocks.)

We live in a world of unfulfilled fairytales.
You were promised I would be dainty
with a size three foot (to fit the glass slipper)
a bell dangling in my skirts,
an apron bow like a present topper
and flowers on my knees
(red and blushing violently).
I was promised you would be tall,
white honored, piney-handed (handy)
golden curled (sweat soaked tendriled)
wearing a coat with three buttons
ruffled feathers beneath,
a popinjay—with a sugar-dusted tongue
and after I tasted you we would fly
into the sun.

Yes,
promises we made
behind the glass.

Housewife

I am peeling the crisp brown suits
off of a pair of onions, reproving
for the clock is digging in
between the ribs and marinade,
it hates the night time sour.

I am broken over the boiling vinegar
and sweet-faced green cucumbers,
knobbed and vulgar, peeled away
to meet their maker.

The house—four rooms with bows tied
end to end to counterfeit the confidence of it
concealed behind draperies
that hemorrhage orange daybreak
onto end tables, side tables, console tables.

Pouring out the one beam
like hot lemon meringue filling
in the blinds, I see it as a slanted scowl,
sad thing, keeping out the
bright, keeping me in, custodian.

She Learns How to Disappear

She memorizes the little spaces she could hide in—
the white place between letters on the page,
the dashboard—a blushing radio throne,
the corner of the yard where crows suckle,
the cherry streetlight which creates the rain,
the white blue sky with its open space
where she could be a splinter in the expanse,
fold up like an origami swan,
tuck her face under her wing, blasphemed.
This one thing is clear, she knows
one more day is purgatory.

Two Young Wives

We two sat
on the swing
on the porch
in the house
by Range lake.

We talked about
the future, which
seemed to end in may.

There—in may—an end.
A bridge between our old lives,
where we were pillars
striving to be wood, strong,
to hold up.
Where we were young,
before thirty rose up
and devoured us,
showing its face
at first in secret places
blue starburst veins,
dimpled smile lines.

Cupping hot cups
of blueberry coffee
we watched yellow oak
and brown pine
and red maple
leaves falling.
They never seemed
to reach the ground,
drifting out over the lake
whose surface was pinched
as if by some invisible touch.

And you remarked,
"I see now how a seed
could be spread across the ocean."

Aerie

Our bones hollow fingertips feather
pinions tinge with gold.
We hide in silver linings quills
line down cotton scrapbook
nests sinews mold the quiet mess
of a body of light—the light of a body.
We soar into flare—burn brighter
burn a hole with a lighter
and view us in it.

The walls built of sheaves of words
the words cleaved from books
the books penned by a sister's hand
the hand tiny and sweet serif finite
sand poured over dead, dry ink.

We remnants of light like sunbeam
hoops petals pressed into walls
like men's mouths who pick
up our light pop it in lick
greasy fingers brush our snow
small and precious off their
charcoal suits.

Jeff Lewis

Charles Ives, a Connecticut Yankee

Kazoo chorus
with flutes, fiddle & flageolets
piccolos, ocarinas & fifes;
                        or: "I heard something else—
there are many roads, you know
besides the Wabash."

The Unanswered Question in a clear Connecticut sky,
a triple hammered to right,
Columbia the Gem of Mutual Life.

                Read in two voice—
                or a battle of the bands,

Giants vs. Cubs	roughly
August, 1907	& in a half-spoken way
Polo Grounds	played as
The Perennial Questions	indistinctly as possible
of Existence,	or gradually excited,

                marginalia
                erasures
                scratches,

all but impossible to decipher The Camp Town Races
in Central Park in the Dark.

Tone roads taken and not taken
are to represent the silence of the druids in Concord.

                Read in two voices
                or tap dance in black face,

Mike jaunts	Watchman, tell us of the night
out to CF.	What the signs of promise are:

Johnny at bat
hits over Mike's head
oboe on the mound
ball strike ball ball
strike
the classic 3 & 2 rhythmic
situation

        Traveler, o'er yon Mt.'s height
        See that Glory-beaming star!

        Watchman, aught of joy or hope?
        Traveler, yes: it brings the day.
        Promised day of Israel
        Dost thou see its beauteous ray?

Music not evolved but mutated
in a sudden paroxysm of Fourth of July!
All Hail the Power!
All Hail the Power!

        Ives, must you hog all the keys?
        Why it's just like a town meeting—
        every man for himself!

Little Richie Wagner,
Pussy Debussy—a Vermont December would do you in,
Mama's boy Mozart,
Chopin the transvestite—

        Jigs gallops reels
        & for every man his own symphony
        & the space to compose it in
        for every man his own Unanswered Questions
        & his own answers in music that sounds like life.

"Stop being such a goddamned sissy!
Stand up for fine, strong music like this
& use your ears like a man!"

Berlioz Wins a Bride

"If she for one moment could conceive all the poetry, all the infinity of a like love, she would fly to my arms though she were to die in my embrace."
—Hector Berlioz

Berlioz, the beautiful hawkman
fell in love with the Muse in the guise of Miss Smithson, the
    Irish actress—
poor Miss Smithson,
poor poor Miss Smithson.

Berlioz pined for her unrequitedly.
Berlioz raved for her Romantically.
Berlioz purple prosed her drunkenly through the suburban
    fields of Paris,
Chopin was concerned for him.

Berlioz saw her embrace her leading man on the stage—
oh fickle Muse, oh fickle fickle Muse!
Oh migraine Muse!
Berlioz ran from the theater weeping to pen his revenge on
    this black lady.

High as a spiraling hawk on opiated hash
Berlioz led her to the dock of Art
where the ragamuffin orchestra judged her:
catcalled its dissonant abuse
Whore! Slut! Scarlet woman!
While Berlioz,
self righteous impresario of the Fantastique,
acting as both conductor and executioner,
dark hair wild,
hawk eyes mad
    started the march to the noose
with a juggle on the tympani
and ended it with the sweet snap of her importunate neck!

But poor Miss Smithson not being Muse cold or Muse true

being flesh and blood did yield to Hector's rude nebulosities
    of love
and did marry him
and there did die in his embrace,
or worse yet turned into an Irish shrew
with an Irish obsession for the booze,
and around and around they went
                              in an accelerando
each with a silver plated pistol
making a witches' Sabbath of the marriage.

He threw her scapula to the rats
hungry for the gory in the music;
she threw his Tuba Mirum to a goat dressed up as the Pope
snarling, "There's your patron!
and here's your Muse!"
Hitching up her skirts to the naked partita
doing a drunken bump and grind,
"Your inspiration, my music box!"

The two of them chopped up the instrument,
gutted the strings,
pulled out the keys like rotted teeth,
hacked off the gangrened pedals
then splintered the body
but the thing kept playing
and playing
its walpurgisnacht
its Totentanz
until she died in the variations.

Poor Miss Smithson,
poor poor Miss Smithson.

Let us imagine his Requiem is for her.

Musak

somewhere in the heartland of the nation, Kansas City say
or maybe Omaha there is a secret underground installation
in this concrete complex buried beneath the stockyards
Musak is rendered from music take a song, any song with
guts and balls   the white smocked Musak technicians cut
it open, sluice out the guts, extract the heroic, send the
remnant to a few symposia on the meaning of "love"   they
pump the resulting comatose thing full of strings, attach
a few angel wings, shoot it up with Hollow Man, then
channel to an ad man composer or poet of hymns to sing
to some king driven mad, centaur being flensed, flautist
having donkey ears attached to his head or great weaver of
Prometheans being turned into a spider
                    "I think that I shall never see a poem as
beautiful as a tree" is how the power of Orpheus came out
of the processing plant "pity this busy monster manunkind
not" the liver of Prometheus after Musak processing "still
falls the rain" the last string of the lyre used as a garrote
"Oh, tannenbaum!" squeaks the tiny voice of Attis from
inside the tree
            lobotomized Eurydice genderless upbeat schlock
Semele so you boogaloo down the aisle not noticing what
demon you're buying as you're shopping 101 Strings
Does the Dismemberment soothes you into missing the
earthquake rising from the casket beneath Kobe
      kill them kill all the songs!
                  or at the dentist's having a root canal
done on your resistance to aliens by the angels humming
Mysterious Mountain
                      kill all the songs!
                            or in the church
where they put you to sleep with A Mighty Fortress so they
can insert Le Sacre du Printemps up your Twentieth Century
      kill all the songs!
                    or on the psych ward taking
your pill of Amahl so you can still give your gifts to the
Kings
            kill all the songs! kill the poor things!

        the hawks with one wing!
                give them the lead gift
                        they're not responsible
and did you know they have Spartacus arranged for the
Mormon Tabernacle Choir?   while Shostakovich's Fourth
Symphony sings in its chains for Rogaine?
                kill all the songs!
                        give them the lead gift in the twilight
kill the poor things!
                        kill all the songs!

Listening to Music

in the evening I drink wine and listen to music
To Copland
Appalachian Spring
"tis a gift to be simple" cranked up loud enough
               so the rocks to hear it
Billy the Kid
bad and proud of it
broke and entered the Muses' Bank
made off with the Genesis account
Shostakovich
the Tenth to keep Stalin dead
Vaughn Williams' Antarctic Symphony
"to forgive wrongs darker than night or death
to suffer woes hope thinks infinite"
and sing it!
not like chains
but like spring!
like, it is not cold here!
it may be cold where you are
shivering in your poetry prisons
but it is not cold here!

it is not cold where I have raised
Prometheus from the bottom of Lake Nancy
I refuse to freeze
beneath a blanket of meekness
in front of a dead fireplace at some church
with the Id Monster chained in the basement

it is before in The Beginning here
when it was good
before Time with his scythe
created that weeping wound
covered by a big popple leaf

I will not repent my life
I will not forget my wife

that I father things
that I have spoken to all the kings
who harden their hearts when Orpheus sings
it is cold on the golf course
where you hide down in Florida!
in *Harpers* where the poem shivers on the page
pawing desperately through Emily Dickinson's under things
searching for a body
trying to build a fire
in the frozen slush pile

after a while the dog in your manger
waiting for a fire builder
will get up
trot off through the woods
toward the source of this music
the real spring

Wagner

Wagner, Mr. Marvel, decided to become a composer
before he could play a single note
so you know he had gall,
balls
with a capital "B."
It must have been playing that angel as a child that did it.

Wagner lived off "impressionable" women for a while
while his creditors plagued him like veritable Walkuries—
he owes them an inspirational debt.

Early on Wagner, like Napoleon, crowned himself
Official Musical Mutant and Composer of the Future.

It was all just in fun, of course
to play Superman,
steal other men's wives
while the queer King of Bavaria
kept you in silks, blank checks
villas and Festspielhaus
so you could fiddle with the Mythos
the dead serious ostinati in the blood,
Schopenhauer's "proto images of the world"
and not laugh when Berlioz quipped
"Yes, Richard, but in Paris we call that digestion, letting a
    little wind."

But the polemics against the Jews
the Aryan hysterics,
the forever Flying Dutchman of your hate
were not "farting," Richard.

As for the Siegfried
we were all spellbound
by the acid trip swastikas in its eyes
before Brunnhilde could destroy the place.

Karen Kraco

Stuck

Infidelity

For the months you've carried this
you've had the wild look of a man
who's been ordered to drive a cab
in a city he doesn't know.
You keep turning: right, right again
but then wrong, wrong, wrong
forgetting to remember that if only you'd ask
I'd show you the map: you might find your way home.

Impasse

A mountain fills the room
and neither of us understands the why
of moving it. Wall-to-wall silence
windows black   doors jammed
cut off from the cities
that twinkle in its valleys.

Irreconcilable

I weep for the speck of the egg
that might have become feathers and cluck
but still can relish the omelet. You, you
crack the shell, see bright red, and swear
off eating eggs for months.
Steaming meals now cold
company no longer invited
silence seated
in the place
of grace.

Postcard Poems: Animal Attitude

Bull

You stick your finger in a can of tuna
then insist the orange cat likes you
for who you are—as flimsy as the red silk cape
you flash in front of your black lab
so proud of your posture
as you call in the picadors!
You knew I was watching
as you dressed down your duck—
webbed footprints up and down
the stairs, across the kitchen floor.

Prairie Dog

Your first line of defense—
go underground. You burrow deep
digging a tangle of tunnels
so that at each choice of paths
I wonder where you've gone.
Once, I did catch up, and instead
of turning to face me, you sat back
on your haunches, blocking the passage,
your arguments lost to me
in the hollowness ahead.
You'll pop up again, I know,
but you won't find me
waiting at your hole.

Roadrunner

How much farther
can you stretch your stress?
Take your taut chicken-neck pulse
then chill. Yesterday, you looked
over your shoulder, ran
without choosing to run
and when you stopped short
no one, not even you, knew.

Whale

What remains unseen
haunts us more
than that flash of black fin
as the water parts.

You surface only
to slip out of my hands
when you sink so deep
that it's too risky to follow.

Watch that bobber drown,
then spring up, wobbling wildly
when it loses the life
to which it's tethered.

Jackalope

You photoshop an effigy of yourself
onto places you'd like to visit

send postcards from everywhere
except where you've been

use some other number
to call the people you love.

When I finally trace you
a total stranger answers, asks

How's he been?

Rough Dreams

Just when you thought it was safe, the cat
in the corner bats rattlesnakes across the room,
and your parakeet, free, sings off-key.

The man for whom you've secretly longed
moves closer, strokes your cheek, and *nyuk, nyuk, nyuks*
like one of the Three Stooges. Get up.
What's that banging at the door?

A neighbor, with an invitation for your goat.
Main course, his mother-in-law's windshield wiper blades.
While you negotiate who will be responsible
for the hoofprints on the hood—you, him, or the goat—

the phone rings.

It's your brother, dead two years today,
wondering what you're going to do
with the clothes still hanging
in the closet: a brown tweed jacket,
his two favorite shirts.

Shaker Village at Pleasant Hill

*The last remaining Shaker at Pleasant Hill,
Sister Mary Settles, died in 1923.*

One baritone sows overtones
of every register.

Brothers here.
                Sisters there.
                              Simple Gifts
      word for word
                    note for note
a's and *o*'s shaped true
        to the way they sang them.

He stamps their beat back
        into the original floorboards.
Steps toward us with open arms,
        broadcasting the smile of every Shaker
                who ever danced in this hall.

Nods greetings to each guest on each bench
        as he walks down the aisle, singing verses
in rhythm that works on us, row by row.
        One by one we offer shy, tight smiles.

A woman in front moans along, monotone.
The couple beside me sways from side to side.
Costume. His rough woven vest is costume, I say,
but I watch two Shakers take his outstretched hands,
then two more, theirs, until the hundreds who we're told
circled and whirled in this empty room grab hands, winding
their way around until we either find ourselves against the wall
or choose to join in.   My foot begins to tap,
longing to belong to this larger thunder.

Three miles away, a farmer lifts his head.

Rafael Miguel Montes

Gas Mask

She's asked me to clean up again.
Asked me to vacuum and dust and mop and,
time permitting,
pull the matted hair stuck to the toilet.
Stiffbrush the mold in the shower stall.

She's asked me this hundreds of Sundays in a row.
As if I might forget.
Perhaps even one day rebel.

I want to damn the toilet all to hell,
make the shower unfit for humans or dogs.
Watch the tiles get black and yellow,
as mold and piss fight for control.
I want this house to smell like a rodeo latrine.

I want my cats stumbling around towers of yellow papers,
torn magazines held up by house corners.
See their furry bodies tangle with bags and bags of Fritos,
a cardboard fort of old pizza boxes,
other cats—caught and killed by my walls of garbage.

I need a team of men in gasmasks gasping "Shit!"
and a tiny woman, in an unthreatening cream suit,
talking about anxiety and "letting go."
Want to have my children crying and screaming,
tell me about a "special" home they plan for me to go,
and how this is the last time and giving up.
Have the youngest one feel guilted into helping.

I want to forget the hair and the dust and the smell,
those things returning every Sunday for me.
I just want to write this poem, now.
I want to clean myself first.

Broom

In just five quick nights, the cinnamon broom
you nailed to the bedroom door
stopped working.

After that excited first unwrap,
we were certain Christmas had come to town.
It was mid-August and we thought we heard carolers.
Tried to remember where we packed the tinsel.
House smelling like pumpkin pie and safety.

Google said cinnamon was a sedative,
a homeopathic peace trigger,
a definitive cure for everyday stress.

We believed her.

Now, the scent is gone.
The broom, still impaled, is just
twigs and knots of wicker.

It looks like we've ripped
some dead stalk from such dry ground.
Splayed the desiccated roots.
Punished it for its exhaustion.

Going Public

I am so done with this private crying,
this dry-eyed staring into space,
this wait for tears to break the drought.

I've become sick of the mechanical swiping
at water rings long ago etched into all this furniture.
Same green rag—same clockwise arc.

Does not matter what the Sears portrait says.
A gone wife ain't coming back into the frame,
a lost boy and a lost girl will not sit still—
here, anymore.

But these nights punching at the mattress,
aimlessly revisioning history,
will stop at sunrise.

Tomorrow, I'm going public with these ghosts.
Do all my crying at the mall.
I'll walk the storefronts redfaced wet,
heave this pain out on a bench in front of Radio Shack.
At the food court, I'll bury my hands in my face,
let the teriyaki congeal around the balls of rice.

When I am ready,
truly ready to let this all go,
I will clutch the handrail to the entrance gate
of the kiddie slide.
Holler out my demons.

Casket

When I was a little boy,
I assumed they nailed coffins shut,
because it would keep away the spiders, the worms.
Keep away the foul-fanged creatures,
feeders of the fat left on the bones.

They nailed it tight.
Only Jesus, the magical carpenter, could pull them out.
He'd remove them sometimes all at once;
sometimes only one nail at a time,
ever ready to change his mind.
Decide to leave you there.

I knew he came for my grandfather and my father,
removed those smooth iron pins,
so bent and caught deep in the wood.
He came to set them free from the ground,
the living dirt still hungry for marrow.

Today, as a grown man,
engine screaming down the highway,
the doors of the panel truck in front of me flew open.
There it was, coming 60 miles an hour at me,
a dark varnished casket, splitting open to the world.

The very moment I swerved,
I did not see its little pink pillow, or a cloudsatin lining.
I did not see the brass handles,
the ones my friends will grab when they carry me to my hole.
When it came at me,
gaping in all its hurtling whiteness,
the very moment I swerved,
I swear I saw teeth.

Mail

My wife receives the most interesting mail.

Last week,
despite my excitement at my "good driver" rebate check,
she was sent four books of poetry,
a postcard from Venice . . . the one in Italy for fuck's sake.

She received three magazines in languages we don't speak,
a pamphlet on growing marijuana . . . unrequested,
two gifts from old students of hers,
and a keychain of the London Eye.

Once,
on the day I got my new Discover card . . . the purple one,
she received a holy Catholic relic,
some saint's microscopic fingernail scrape,
embedded in a Swarovski crystal rosary.

When we're both dead,
whoever finds this box of junk mail,
the one I've been keeping balanced on the printer,
will know I was staid.
Serious.
A rectangle of nothing with a silly decorative stamp.

They'll know I was one of life's unnecessary calendars,
some charity's mass-run reward for my sucker check.
They'll know my overwhelming fear of making noise,
my paralyzing quiet.

But when they reach your bedside.
Oh, the glorious things they'll find.
You, my dear, you'll be the gypsy heart,
the insane tumult of the world in carnival spin.
They will know you've been a saint,
a reveler, a traveler, a slut.
They will know you were my voice.

Contributor Notes

Melissa Bond never was a skinny girl, always was a small girl, always had to jump. It started here, with brooding and a Jim Morrison crush, big as a movie. She writes a chapbook called *Hush* to talk about addiction, the slosh and snuff that nearly rubbed her out. She writes about Freud and drugs and the child that came, fast as a speedball—the one with an extra chromosome. She wins awards. She keeps writing.

Micah Chatterton lives in Riverside, California. Read more at micahchatterton.com

Charles C. Childers is a writer based out of Huntington, WV. Graduating from Marshall University with degree in English (emphasis in literary studies), he aspires to someday get a graduate degree in comparative literature. Interests include: Zen and Taoism, bouts of social drinking, hiking the hillsides of his home state, raising fancy rats, general hell-raising and environmental advocacy.

Erin Dorso is an educator and poet living in Walla Walla, Washington with her husband and two children. She has taught language arts in Florida, Japan, and Washington and now develops professional learning for other educators in her region. Her poetry is inspired by the natural world, at home and on the road.

Laurel Eshelman writes from Elizabeth, Illinois, population 700, and works a few blocks from home at the family business, Eshelman Pottery. Her chapbook, *The Red Mercy*, was a semi-finalist in the 2014 Palettes and Quills Chapbook Contest. Laurel's poems and essays have appeared in her chapbook, *The Scale of Things*, in *Love from Galena*, *The Phoenix Soul*, *Sweet & Saucy* and *The Prairie Wind*.

Michael Fleming was born in San Francisco, raised in Wyoming, and has lived and learned and worked all around the world, from Thailand, England, and Swaziland to Berkeley, New York City, and now Brattleboro, Vermont. He's been a teacher, a grad student, a carpenter, and always a writer; for the past decade he has edited literary anthologies for W. W. Norton. Read more at www.dutchgirl.com/foxpaws

Susan F. Glassmeyer is a on the Poetry Diet, grazing all day long. She has two chapbooks available: *Body Matters* (Pudding House Publications, 2010) and *Cook's Luck* (Finishing Line Press, 2012). Susan is the founder of Little Pocket Poetry and "April Gifts" at www.LittlePocketPoetry.org. Ms. Glassmeyer is a somatic therapist and co-director of the Holistic Health Center in Cincinnati, Ohio.

Emily Graf currently resides in Austin, Texas, where she enjoys coffee and oranges in a sunny chair. She graduated from Kenyon College in 2015 with a degree in English & Poetry Writing. Her work has been previously published in Maudlin House, Right Hand Pointing, and elsewhere, online and in print.

Colby Hansen lives and works in Denver. He studied English at Portland's Reed College and, later, elementary education at the University of Colorado at Boulder. He now teaches third grade. Most of his projects, including the novel-in-verse he's currently soliciting for publication, are for kids. Although he's been writing for the last fifteen years, this is his first time in print.

Karen Kraco lives in Minneapolis, where she teaches high-school chemistry. Over the years she has alternated teaching gigs with stints as an editor and freelance writer. Her profiles, feature articles, and poems have appeared in local and regional publications, and she was co-editor and publisher of the poetry journal *ArtWord Quarterly*.

Jeff Lewis has a Master's Degree in Fine Arts, painting, from the University of WI, Superior. I have had poems published in *The Wisconsin Academy Review*, *San Jose Studies*, *Magical Blend*, *Kansas Quarterly*, and other magazines. I am a five-time winner of the Lake Superior Writers Award for poetry. I am married, have two children and live in Northwestern Wisconsin.

Kate Magill is a Vermont native and a devoted backcountry wanderer. This is her second appearance in *Sixfold*. Her first volume of poetry, *Roadworthy Creature, Roadworthy Craft*, was published in 2011 by Fomite Press.

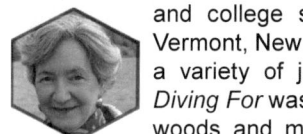

Linda Sonia Miller I have been a teacher of kindergarten and college students, teachers and incarcerated youth in Vermont, New York and Connecticut. My work has appeared in a variety of journals, and my chapbook *Something Worth Diving For* was published in 2012. I am inspired to write by the woods and mountains among which I live, the increasingly incomprehensible political landscape, and the revelations that come from a life spent among children.

Rafael Miguel Montes, born in Santiago de Cuba, is a Cultural Studies professor at St. Thomas University and a Cuban-American writer living and working in Miami. His literary work reflects his dual upbringing in the Cuban-American community of Hialeah, Florida, and the academic communities of a number of institutions of higher learning. Twice nominated for a Pushcart award in poetry, his writing has appeared in *The Caribbean Writer*, *The New York Quarterly*, *Tattoo Highway*, *Conclave: A Journal of Character*, *Magnapoets*, *Criminal Class*, *Prole* (UK), and a number of other academic and literary journals. His poem "Menu" won the 2011 UK Poetry Kit Award for best poem in an independent literary journal.

Barry W. North is a seventy-one-year-old retired refrigeration mechanic. He was born and raised in New Orleans and presently lives with his wife, Diane, in Hahnville, Louisiana. Since his retirement in 2007, he has been nominated twice for a Pushcart Prize, won the A. E. Coppard Prize for Fiction, and was recently named a finalist in the 2014 Lascaux Poetry Awards. He has had three chapbooks published. For more information please visit his website, www.barrynorth.org

Richard Parisio has worked as an interpretive naturalist for over forty years, in the Everglades, Pocono Mountains, at Assateague Island, and, since 1984, in the Catskills and Hudson valley. He is currently NYS Coordinator for *River of Words*, a national children's poetry and art contest on the theme of watersheds. His poetry collection, *The Owl Invites Your Silence*, won the 2014 Slapering Hol Press Poetry Chapbook Contest.

Ricky Ray was born in Florida and educated at Columbia University. In 2013, he received the Ron McFarland poetry prize, and second-prize in the Whisper River poetry contest. In 2015, he won a Cormac McCarthy write-alike contest. He has performed alongside such luminaries as Saul Williams. He lives in Manhattan with his wife, three cats and a dog, where they dream of farm life in an undiscovered village.

Cassandra Sanborn studied creative writing at Purdue University and now lives in Indianapolis, Indiana. This is her second publication in *Sixfold*.

Jane Schulman is a poet and short story writer. She also works as a speech pathologist in a Brooklyn public school with young children with autism and significant cognitive delays. Jane has been a featured poet in local venues and taught senior citizens to write their lives in poetry, fiction, and memoir.

A born and bred Oklahoman, Jennifer Leigh Stevenson loves the backroads. She began writing poetry in ninth grade, studied music and theater at University of Central Oklahoma and wound up (somehow) in banking. For years she scribbled lines on napkins and wrote rhymes on the back of receipts, until she realized she wanted to be a writer more than anything. This marks Jennifer's second time to be published in *Sixfold*.

J. Lee Strickland is a freelance writer living in upstate New York. In addition to fiction, he has written on the subjects of rural living, modern homesteading and voluntary simplicity. His work has appeared or is forthcoming in *Sixfold, Atticus Review, Icarus Down Review, Latchkey Tales, Garlic Press, Countryside, Small Farm Journal*, and others. He is a member of the Mohawk Valley Writers' Group and The Hudson Valley Writers Guild.

Melissa Tyndall is a writer, bibliophile, caffeine addict, professor, and Supernatural fangirl. She holds a Bachelor of Science in English, a Master of Arts in Corporate Communication, and Master of Fine Arts in Creative Writing. Her poems and award-winning articles have appeared in *Number One, Prism international, Red Mud Review, Words + Images*, and various newspapers. Her work is forthcoming in an essay collection examining The CW television series *Supernatural*. She lives in Nashville, Tennessee.

Holly Lyn Walrath attended the University of Texas at Austin for her BA in English and the University of Denver for her MLA in Creative Writing. She is a freelance editor and the Associate Director of Writespace, a nonprofit literary center in Houston, Texas. Her work has appeared or is forthcoming in *The Vestal Review, Literary Orphans*, and *Pulp Literature*, among others. Find her at hlwalrath.com or @hollylynwalrath

J.H Yun is a Korean-American poet, currently completing her MFA at New York University. Her work has appeared or is forthcoming in *Narrative*, *AAWW The Margins*, *Prelude*, and elsewhere.

Made in the USA
Thornton, CO
01/19/24 13:57:09

8c27a941-80c3-484f-9c2c-2b0eb5132355R01